# Learning the Hidden Curriculum

# Learning the Hidden Curriculum:
## The Odyssey of One Autistic Adult

**Judy Endow, MSW**

**Foreword by Brenda Smith Myles, PhD**

# FUTURE HORIZONS

www.fhautism.com
info@fhautism.com
817.277.0727

Publisher's Cataloging-in-Publication

Endow, Judy.

    Learning the hidden curriculum : the odyssey of one autistic adult / Judy Endow ; foreword by Brenda Smith Myles.

      p. ; cm.

    ISBN: 978-1-934575-93-2
    LCCN: 2012931261
    Includes bibliographical references.

    1. Autistic people--Life skills guides. 2. Social skills--Study and teaching. 3. Autistic people--Personal narratives. I. Title.

RC553.A88 E63 2012
616.85/882--dc23                                1202

As this book was getting ready to go to press, I had the honor and privilege, together with Mom, to be at Dad's side as he readied himself for his one last journey. Today my sorrow is fresh; I can't imagine how we will ever get along without him. And yet, I am comforted in knowing readers will meet a glimpse of my dad as they read this book. I am lucky to have had passed down to me my dad's sense of humor.

As his life wound down and he needed more and more care, he never lost his sense of humor. I will always remember him jingling change in his pocket as he walked around, his courage to face life despite many health problems, his strong love for his wife and family and, most of all, his ability to find the humor in everyday ordinary life.

And thus, I dedicate this book to my dad:

Delmar "Del" Linders
Born: May 19, 1931
Died: January 2, 2012

# Table of Contents

# Foreword

**W**hen I look back to when and how Judy and I met and the events that transpired afterward, I am surprised that she became and remains a good friend. I was her fifth friend, and Judy told me very frankly that she didn't know if she could handle the demands of having a fifth friend and having *me* as a friend. My life is not predictable; it is some-times fast paced; and is always multifaceted – I multitask and change tasks, sometimes in mid-sentence.

Judy and I spend approximately two weeks together each year. We each look forward to this time – usually we work on a project, such as writing a book or a calendar, but manage to plan a myriad activities that often leave us marveling over a piece of artwork or laughing about absolutely nothing.

I am proud to say that I introduced Judy to the hidden curriculum[1]; and equally proud to say that she introduced me to a different way of thinking and reflecting. We accommodate each other's working and living style – she likes to start work *early* in the morning with no disruptions. I like to start a bit later (I don't believe that there are two 5 o'clocks in one day!) and actually like interruptions. So when I am ready to work, she is ready to talk. I hate to unload the dishwasher and Judy hates for me to unload it – because I am too loud. She listens to my "half-baked" ideas and I listen to hers. We fit nicely together.

Judy's odyssey through the hidden curriculum has been amazing. She has been fearless in attempting to understand the hidden curriculum and broaden her world by using this newfound knowledge. For example, in the few years that I have known her, Judy has managed to learn how to navigate international travel, respond to literally a hundred people who want to interact with her personally at a conference, arrange, with her mother, for the care of her medically fragile dad in his final days, respond to a standing ovation, master texting and PowerPoint animation to a degree that I never will, determine whose intentions are good and identify those who do not mean her well, and so much more. She faces life head on – viewing each hidden curriculum item as a key to opening the world a bit more.

---

1 Apple & King, 1977; Jackson, 1968; Kanpol, 1989; LaVoie, 1994; Myles, Trautman, & Schelvan, 2004.

# Foreword

All this has taken great diligence on Judy's part – not only does she identify that a hidden curriculum item exists, but she strives to understand all aspects. This is not an easy task. There is so much that is hidden. Recently, Judy upgraded to first class on a flight because she had mileage to do so. This was her first venture in first class and she didn't know the hidden curriculum. To understand how difficult the hidden curriculum can be to master, I have presented the text messages that we sent back and forth on first class protocol.

J: HELP. Upgraded to 1st class. What do I need to know?

B: You board first. And you will be well taken care of. You will probably be offered extra food and drinks. They will also offer to hang up your coat. First class has its own bathroom.

J: Already boarded. Love the extra room! Been asked if I want a drink. I said no because I wasn't sure of the protocol.

B: You can say yes to a drink as many times as you wish.

J: I don't see a bathroom.

B: It is in the front.

J: What are the choices? Am I allowed to ask or am I meant to know?

B: Choice?

J: Drinks.

B: You can ask what they have. Also, drinks are usually listed in the back of the airline magazine in the seat pocket in front of you. I would suggest asking.

J:  Good to know.

B:  You can also request a drink by saying, "May I have something to drink?"

J:  1. Figure out where the bathroom is. 2. Drink. Genius woman! Was going to ask if there was a special button to push for requesting a drink.

B:  No light for the drink, but perhaps one for the bathroom. There might be a sign in the center near the front of the plane. Look for a flat door – that's the bathroom. Not the one where the pilot sits.

J:  Is it okay to ask the flight attendant when she comes by where the bathroom is? Don't want to look too much like Sheldon here (from *The Big Bang Theory*).

B:  Of course. You can also raise your hand slightly and say, "Excuse me" to get her attention.

J:  Which hand?

B:  Doesn't matter. This is the same protocol for getting a waiter's attention at a restaurant.

J:  Ohhhhh that is good to know. After all of this, you know I really am not hungry or thirsty! Well, a new experience for me. Thanks a bunch! Time to power down.

B:  ☺

This book is very important. Not only does it talk about the hidden curriculum, it also addresses how to take hidden information and generalize it to other settings. Judy is simply brilliant! You will see this for yourself when you read this book.

– Brenda Smith Myles, PhD

# References

Apple, M. W., & King, N. R. (1977). What do schools teach? *Curriculum Inquiry, 6*(4), 341-358.

Jackson, P. (1968). *Life in classrooms.* New York, NY: Holt, Rinehart, & Winston.

Kanpol, B. (1989). Do we dare teach some truths? An argument for teaching more 'hidden curriculum.' *College Student Journal, 23,* 214-217.

LaVoie, R. (1994). Learning disabilities and social skills with Richard LaVoie. In J. Bieber (Ed.), *Last one picked ... first one picked on.* Washington, DC: Public Broadcasting Service.

Myles, B. S., Trautman, M. L., & Schelvan, R. L. (2004). *The hidden curriculum: Practical solutions for understanding unstated rules in social situations.* Future Horizons.

The "hidden curriculum" refers to the set of
rules or guidelines that are often not directly
taught but are assumed to be known (Garnett,
1984; Hemmings, 2000; Jackson, 1968; Kanpol,
1989). The hidden curriculum contains items
that impact social interactions, school per-
formance, and sometimes safety. The hidden
curriculum also includes idioms, metaphors,
and slang – things most people "just pick up"
or learn through observation or subtle cues,
including body language. (Myles, Trautman, &
Schelvan, 2004, p. 5)

# Introduction

**A** few years back I had a conversation with Brenda
Myles about her work on the hidden curriculum. As a
person with autism, I very much appreciated the hidden curriculum items in the annual calendars that were based on her
work. It was wonderful to read these calendars, but while I
gained new information, the problem was that the items were
directed at children. I needed something that would speak to
situations in my own life as an adult.

I suspected that not understanding the hidden curriculum was
the culprit messing me up socially and was hoping to encour-
age Brenda to come up with a hidden curriculum calendar
addressing adult hidden social rules. But instead of granting my
wish, Brenda replied that I was better suited to write such a calendar than she was, and she proceeded to invite me to do so.

At the time, I felt very ill suited to the task … how was it that
an over-50 autistic adult who recognizes she doesn't under-

stand the hidden curriculum well enough to get along effectively in social situations was all of a sudden in a position to author something she didn't understand? And yet, that is exactly what happened!

From that point on, whenever we were together, as they came up, Brenda would point out the hidden curriculum items that tripped me up. In the beginning, I learned the items as they were pointed out to me. I wrote them down, and soon I had the start of the first year of hidden curriculum calendar items for older adolescents and adults.

Over time, I became able to identify *after the fact* – after I had made a social faux pas – that my failure to understand the hidden curriculum was to blame, even though I couldn't yet figure out exactly which hidden curriculum item had tripped me up. After much trial and error, and great mindfulness, I have now reached a point where I am able at least to relay the situation to somebody else and, with that person's help, figure out the to-me-unknown social information that had resulted in the behavior that had created a poor social outcome for me.

As I continued this process, watching my conversation partners closely, intentionally noticing and tracking their body language, I discovered after a while that people gave off tell-tale looks immediately after I committed a social error. They often got a question-mark look on their face, scrunching their eyebrows together and downwards while moving their head slightly backwards. Some sighed and/or rolled their eyes, sometimes just slightly and other times a bit more dramatically. Often they would abruptly change the conversation topic or find a way to end the conversation and walk away.

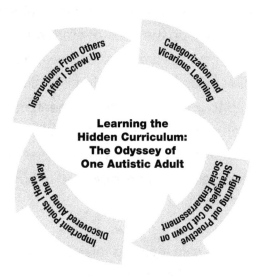

I got quite good at recognizing this body language and at understanding that whatever I had said immediately prior to the onset of these sorts of "red flags" was tied to a social error I had committed due to my failure to understand some item of the hidden curriculum that most everyone else my age understood more or less automatically.

This was a helpful step, but I wanted to figure out how to know the missing information *before* committing the "social sin" (term used by Grandin & Barron, 2005), and thus avoid the negative social consequences. This posed quite a dilemma! After all, how can you figure out what it is you don't know when, in fact, you don't know it? I complained about this to Brenda and often told her I wanted to "crack the code."

Now, three years later, I know lots more about the hidden curriculum. In fact, once I got a Blackberry that traveled with me everywhere, I took up the habit of emailing myself newly discovered hidden curriculum items as they came up in my daily life. The first calendar I completed is mainly filled with items others had to point out to me. As mentioned, typically, this happened after the fact. That is, I had already "sinned" and only learned the hidden-to-me information after having made a fool of myself, or worse, offended or hurt somebody's feelings.

This way of learning also involved relying on others to point out my errors – not an entirely comfortable position to be in. But the good news is that I did learn, proof being that I had compiled more items than needed for the next calendar a month ahead of the deadline. Then, in about another six months, I again had more than enough items for another hidden curriculum calendar – way ahead of even being officially asked to write it.

The feedback on the two calendars was very positive, but my publisher decided that rather than continuing to publish collections of hidden curriculum items that readers more or less had to memorize and then hope they would be able to retrieve when appropriate, a more useful tool would combine

individual items with a way to learn to discover one's own –
the way I had been able to do over the years.

This book does just that. It includes many entirely new items
along with some items from the 2010 and 2011 calendars.
But rather than simply being a list of items, it presents my
three-year journey of bringing intentionality to learning the
hidden curriculum as it relates to my life as a 50-something-
year-old autistic woman.

My life has become easier as I have come into more and more
social understanding. Even though each person will travel his or
her own journey in learning the hidden curriculum, I hope that
outlining my experiences thus far will help other autistics and
those who love, support and live with them.

This book is organized to reflect the major stages I went
through when I set out to intentionally figure out how to learn
the elusive hidden curriculum – Instruction From Others After
I Screw Up, Categorization and Vicarious Learning, Figuring
out Proactive Strategies to Cut Down on Social Embarrassment, and Important Points I've Discovered Along the Way.
Further, the discussion in each chapter is accompanied by
examples of relevant hidden curriculum items with activities
scattered throughout as suggestions for how readers may try
to apply the lessons I have learned to their own lives.

**Chapter One:**

# Instruction From Others After I Screw Up

W hen I started on my odyssey to deliberately learn the hidden curriculum, my primary means of gathering hidden curriculum items was to have others point it out to me *after* I made a social error. Up until this time in my life, even though I was very talkative with individual people, I was rarely talkative in groups, especially if I didn't know someone in the group well. I made social blunders so often that I found it more comfortable not to be a social sort of person. That way, I figured, I would not risk the embarrassment that was bound to come when I made a blunder in front of someone who didn't know me well.

Part of this decision was to protect my professional life. I know how much first impressions count and realize how incompetent I can appear when I make social blunders. In practical terms, this means that it is better for me to keep my mouth shut in front of strangers than to risk making a negative first impression. After all, you only have one chance to make a first impression, and I wanted that to be a good one.

Knowing the potential for committing social blunders, I relied on my close friends to point out to me – after the fact – the errors I was making. With these friends I knew that when I made a social "miss-step," not only would they let me know, they would keep on being my friends. We are free to be ourselves with each other. The more I hang out with these friends, the more opportunities I will have to discover new hidden curriculum items.

## Making Mistakes in the Community

Writing the hidden curriculum calendars enticed me to become a socially braver person. One thing I did as part of this resolve was to become a houseguest for a couple of weeks on different occasions at the home of Brenda Myles. During my visits, Brenda and I would work most of the day and then usually go somewhere afterwards. We ran everyday errands, visited art galleries, got massages, and generally, were out and about in the community enjoying each other's company.

In the process, I learned many hidden curriculum items, and Brenda had many opportunities to clue me in. The best part was that we both could be ourselves and have fun at the same time. Perhaps the results of our time together should not be that much of a surprise! After all, Brenda is an international expert on autism and noted for applying the hidden curriculum concepts to the field of autism. I am an author and an autistic adult trying to learn enough hidden curriculum items to fill up a page a day calendar. Put us together and ta-da – the first calendar was off to a good start!

Here are the hidden curriculum items I learned while out in the community. Many are a direct result of my visits with Brenda. Others are the result of being out and about with other close friends. In all of these instances, I learned the hidden curriculum item because my friends were gracious enough to clue me in after I made a social blunder.

## Hidden Curriculum Items: Community Outings

- Even though the smell of certain stores makes you nauseated, it is better not to announce it to your friend while in the store. Instead, say you are stepping out to get some fresh air.

- If you see a fat person exercising, it will not be perceived as encouragement to tell him, "Good for you to be exercising. You really need it!"

- When waiting to load your items on the conveyor belt at the grocery store checkout, it is considered a social sin to rearrange another customer's items so as to take up less space, thus making room for your own items.

- "Rolling hills" actually do not roll. They are usually several small stationary hills, one after the other, that give the illusion of movement when you look at them.

- People are not meant to sing along to the background music playing in malls.

- It is impolite to pull out your phone and start texting or make a call when having dinner with a friend. If for an emergency reason you need to receive a phone or text message during the meal, explain this ahead of time.

- Some stores that sell bath products or perfumes have strong odors. It is fine to notice the odor, but it is rude to walk in and announce, "It stinks in here."

- It is O.K. if somebody uses the antibacterial wipes located by shopping carts for a different use, even though they are meant to wipe off the shopping cart handles. It is not necessary to report this to the store manager.

- Even though it is true, if someone is giving you a ride, it is best not to tell him how dirty his car looks or to make any negative comments about his car as it would make you appear rude and ungrateful.

- Some shopping mall food courts don't have enough seating for all the customers, especially during busy times. If you need to sit in order to eat, look around before you purchase your food to determine if there are empty tables to ensure you will have a place to sit.

**ACTIVITY:** Make a deal with a trusted friend who understands the hidden curriculum to go somewhere in the community together, such as to the mall or out to eat, and during the time together do not inhibit anything. The purpose is to allow all your thoughts to be spoken so that your friend can help you decipher the unknown-to-you hidden curriculum. For example, once I had made a deal with a friend not to inhibit before going to the mall. Because of this deal, I didn't inhibit and thus sang along to the background music as I normally did when I was alone in the mall. Hearing me, my friend was able to tell me that singing along to the background music was something people do not usually do and that it made me look "different" and drew attention to me in a negative way.

# Clues That Instruction Is About to Be Delivered

While spending time out in the community with close friends with whom I did not feel the need to inhibit my comments, one thing I became aware of was that my friends were predictable in letting me know when instruction was about to be delivered. They consistently used certain phrases, such as ...

- I shouldn't have to tell you, but ...
- It should be obvious that ...
- Everyone knows ...
- Common sense tells us ...
- No one ever ... (Myles et al., 2004, p. 5)

It was helpful for me to learn these key phrases because many people say things like this before giving important hidden curriculum instruction, but few tell you that the information they are about to give pertains to a hidden curriculum rule of society. These statements are like a secret code meaning, "Here comes a hidden curriculum item." On the following page is a sample of hidden curriculum items I have encountered preceding the delivery of instruction after I had already screwed up socially.

## Hidden Curriculum Items: "Everybody Knows ..."

- If you bring a cooler with cold drinks to the beach, it is polite to offer those in your party a cold drink if you have extras.

- When people ask, "Why am I not surprised?" it is a rhetorical question, meaning no answer is needed or expected. Such a question is used to communicate the person is not actually surprised because he or she could have anticipated whatever happened.

- Some people have more friends than others. Most people do not know the exact number of friends they have. It is fine not to know exactly how many friends you have.

- Gossip is when you repeat information someone has told you about another person. It is best not to make a habit of repeating this kind of second-hand information.

- Sometimes people are very interested in learning their family history. If a friend or relative is attending a genealogy meeting, it does not mean they value dead people over living people. It has nothing to do with you or your friendship.

- A dog on a leash wearing a red vest in a public place where dogs are not normally allowed is likely a service dog. Service dogs are generally allowed to accompany their owners in places where pets are otherwise not allowed.

- Saying, "Excuse me" after passing gas in public draws attention to the fact that you did it. Unless it is obvious that you are the culprit, it is better to keep quiet.

- Many advertisements for fad diets use people who claim phenomenal results. In reality, even though the people in the ads sound quite believable, the results for most people are less than the claims.

- Most of the time, exercise equipment sold on television infomercials use actors and actresses to sell the equipment. It is highly unlikely that your body will look like theirs no matter how much you use the particular piece of exercise equipment.

- It is rare to win more money than you put into a gambling machine. Wise people don't plan on winning, but decide ahead how much money they are willing to spend for the entertainment. If they happen to win, they consider it an exciting bonus.

# Learning From the Mean, Negative Reactions of Others

For a long time, the only way I was able to learn the hidden curriculum was to depend on my friends to explain it to me after I had made a social error or wait for what was often a monumentally embarrassing situation where strangers berated or yelled at me. Lots of times I have found myself in very embarrassing situations due to my failure to understand the hidden curriculum.

For example, one day in the bakery department of my grocery store I saw a sign next to a plate of cookies that read, "Free Cookies." I thought it was a nice gesture on the part of the bakery department and promptly slid all the cookies off the plate into the plastic produce bag holding a lemon that was in my shopping cart. A few moments later, the bakery lady chased me down shouting, "What is wrong with you?" She then proceeded to call me some derogatory names and said, "What kind of pig takes ALL the cookies?"

I had my young children with me and felt awful at having them hear the bakery lady calling me a pig. Her shouting made me realize that even though the word "cookies" was plural on the sign, the plate of cookies was intended to follow the rules of grocery store samples: One Per Customer. I did not know what to do in the moment, so I blurted out, "What am I supposed to do?" She just told me, "Keep the damn cookies, but don't you ever try this trick again!" I switched grocery stores and never went back to that store due to my embarrassment.

Here is a list of items I learned because somebody either yelled at me or in some other negative way put me "in my place" after I inadvertently committed a social sin because I did not understand the hidden curriculum.

## Hidden Curriculum Items: "What's Wrong With You?"

- Don't take your shoes off in public places unless everyone else is doing it, such as at a swimming pool or beach.

- In elevators you do not need to figure out if the combined body weight of the passengers exceeds the weight limit posted. Weight limits are posted as a guideline for heavy cargo.

- If a person raises his hand in the motion of a stop cue, it means you should immediately stop what you are saying. It's best to wait a few moments to see what happens next.

- Occasionally, an automatic flush toilet in a public restroom will fail to flush. There is not much you can do about it. Just exit the stall as if the toilet had flushed.

- Children sometimes pee in public swimming pools. There are usually enough chemicals in the pool to eliminate any health risk.

- On occasion, you will see a mother nursing a baby in a public place. You might glance at this but do not stare. Also, it is not necessary to make any comments.

- At a cinema showing several movies, you must purchase a separate ticket for each movie you would like to see.

- When a tall person sitting in front of you blocks your view at an event, do not tell the person to move. If possible you may relocate and, if not, you are expected to accept the situation no matter how much you hate it.

- When public places are crowded, such as at a beach or in an airport, people generally do not enter into other parties' conversations just because they can easily hear what is being said.

- Even though you may be trying to be helpful, do not walk over and pick food out of a man's beard unless that man is a close friend, relative, or your significant other.

# Learning From the Nonverbal Reactions of Others

As part of this odyssey, I wanted to avoid the sort of public embarrassment that happens when somebody corrects by yelling at me or in some way humiliates me because they assume my behavior is based on intentional disregard for social convention. Even though my behavior may look rude, rudeness is rarely my intention. I hated it when others would assume rudeness or ascribe intentionality to my oblivious-to-me social mistakes. I wanted to learn the hidden information that would inform me before I made the social mistake, but at times it seemed impossible. There are so many variables! I realized that I would likely literally die before I learned enough individual hidden curriculum items to enable me to not be so anxious about committing daily social blunders. After all, here I was – over 50 years old – and this knowledge still was not coming to me automatically.

But then one day I noticed something new was happening! I was still committing lots of social sins, but *without being told*, I was beginning to recognize when I had committed a social sin. This meant I was having feelings of embarrassment due to people's reactions to my behavior. It seemed like a miracle that I could now put this all this together. But even though I knew it was a big positive change for me, it didn't feel good. It felt terrible.

In fact, having regular feelings of embarrassment because of my behavior was depressing. Many days I just wanted to hide at home and not even try to interact with people. I had to do lots of positive self-talk, reminding myself I wasn't intentionally setting out to be a bad person or a social misfit but was beginning to understand after the fact that I had committed a social sin because I could now read others' reactions to my behavior.

I realized that I had a choice to make. I could either go back to being a social recluse, engaging less with people and giving up on this idea of trying to learn the hidden curriculum. Or I could keep on keeping on – getting out there interfacing with people in the community, knowing I was learning, as evidenced by the fact that I now could become embarrassed after my bad behavior *without needing anyone to explain it to me.*

Even though I often felt bad, I determined I would keep going because I had nothing to lose and only more to learn. So, I became more determined than ever in my pursuit to figure this out for myself.

The following items are examples of hidden curriculum I was able to figure out based on embarrassing feelings I experienced after committing a social error.

## Hidden Curriculum Items: "I Know That Look!"

- If you see two people arguing in a public place, do not tell them to stop arguing. In fact, don't even talk to them even if your intention is to be helpful.

- Some restaurant menus show pictures of food items. Know that the food served rarely looks exactly like the picture shown in the menu.

- All who wish may join in congregational singing in church. It is not necessary to be a good singer to participate. Just sing quietly so as to blend in with the other singers.

- It is best to inhibit repeated sounds of fear or surprise in a movie theater if your reaction doesn't match the voiced experience of other moviegoers, so as not to become annoying to those around you.

- When you are asked if you know where something is located such as the library or courthouse, the person asking the question is usually asking for directions. If you know where the place is located go ahead and give the directions rather than answering the question with a "yes."

- Do not blow your nose on dinner napkins. Use a tissue.

- If you want a friend to put something on a jump drive (also referred to as thumb drive and USB stick) it doesn't turn out well to say, "Put that up your stick." For some reason people think it is a rude way to speak.

- If you can't remember something polite to say in a social situation, don't ask the person you are with. For example, when served dinner at a friend's home, don't ask, "What is a polite thing to say when you hate the food being served?"

- While it is a good idea to wear warm outerwear such as gloves and hats during cold winter months, this is a personal choice. It's not polite to insist that others wear gloves and hats even if your intent is to make sure they are comfortable in the cold weather.

- Most people have experienced the panicked feeling of thinking their car has been stolen from a public parking lot. This usually means you have lost your bearings and are looking in the wrong area of the lot. Search around a bit before reporting the car stolen. You will likely locate your car.

## Chapter Two:

# Categorization and Vicarious Learning

As time went on, I had more and more experiences, in a variety of circumstances, where I intentionally did not inhibit my comments. Once I started, it seemed that I was able to learn more and more hidden curriculum items at an increasing rate, but my learning still was tied to another person. I still did not feel comfortable saying whatever came to mind around others, unless I was with one of a handful of my special friends. I was still nervous about screwing up. I knew that when I made social blunders, these particular friends would not think any less of me as a human being but would just fill in the information I needed to learn.

The unfortunate thing for most of us on the autism spectrum is that we don't always have a trusted friend around when we make social blunders. The results can range from mildly embarrassing to totally catastrophic. In my professional life, besides speaking on a variety of autism topics, I consult with school districts and agencies on behalf of individuals with autism. I didn't want to make mistakes that would negatively affect my work life. I knew of several unfortunate circumstances of autistics who have lost jobs and who have even been jailed after behaving in a manner that disregarded hidden curriculum rules.

Around this time, the 2010 Hidden Curriculum Calendar for Older Adolescents and Adults was nearly ready to go to print. The last thing I was asked to do was to provide a topical index for the calendar items. This was much more difficult for me than I imagined. Categorization was difficult. It is not something my brain seems to do naturally.

To help myself to come up with categories, I looked at how others had broken down the hidden curriculum and created categories. I looked at the kids' calendars (Myles, 2006; Myles & Duncan 2007, 2008) and also read things by other adult autistics, such as *The Unwritten Rules of Social Relationships* (Grandin & Barron, 2005).

This was not only helpful for me to complete the task at hand – constructing the topical index – it was also helpful in terms of taming the huge mass of hidden curriculum items I had now gathered in my head. Learning to put items into categories was helpful because I no longer had thousands of items to keep track of, but instead had clumps (or categories) of general headings where I could find individual items. It was a relief to have ways to sort and categorize items, and it made me less anxious.

## Memorizing the "Illegal" Category

Not all social sins are equally bad, but some are SO bad that they get a person in serious trouble. Not understanding this "bad" list of hidden curriculum items can have significant negative impact on our lives. For example, one young man ended up with serious problems because he didn't understand that looking into the window of his friend's apartment building would get him into trouble.

When Pete and Greg were growing up, Pete would ring the doorbell of Greg's home when he went to visit. If nobody answered the door, Pete would tap on the window, cup his hands around his eyes, put his face up to the window and look in to see if Greg was home. This worked for Pete all through high school. Greg did not respond to the doorbell, but when he heard Pete tapping on the window and peering in, he would open the door for Pete. This was O.K. while Greg was living in the family home.

After high school, Greg and Pete both received county support services that enabled them to move out of their family homes. Going to visit at Greg's new apartment for the first time, Pete rang Greg's doorbell, and when nobody answered, as was his habit, he rapped on the front window and peered in. But Pete was no longer peering into the window of Greg's family home where everybody knew him. Instead, it was the window of the downstairs tenant in Greg's new apartment building. Also, Pete was no longer a child, but had grown into a man.

In response to a phone call from the downstairs tenant, the police arrived, and promptly handcuffed and arrested Pete. The fact that circumstances had changed and what was once O.K. behavior was now illegal was something Pete did not know. Pete's social misstep in this situation was very serious because his behavior, permissible as a child, was illegal now that he was an adult.

We cannot depend on others to respond to our social missteps in the same way our trusted friends do. Besides, even though I could depend on my friends when they were with me, they were not always with me, such as when I was working, doing errands and generally living my life. There are certain behaviors that as an autistic I just needed to memorize so as never to commit a social hidden curriculum sin that would result in legal trouble.

Here is the start of a list of hidden curriculum items that can have negative legal ramifications.

## Hidden Curriculum Items: Police/Legal List

- Don't make threatening remarks in public. Even if you don't mean what you say, you could find yourself in serious legal trouble if the remarks are taken seriously.*

- Some traffic lights have cameras mounted on them that automatically take a picture of vehicles crossing the intersection on a red light. A ticket is then mailed to the person to whom the vehicle is registered, and this person is responsible for paying the ticket.

- Don't make verbal threats in public or at work. Even if you don't mean literally what you say, when adults make threats, it can easily become a criminal matter. (HCCAA 2011)

- Never joke about doing something illegal such as bombing a building or robbing a bank. You could be taken seriously and, if so, find yourself in legal trouble. (HCCAA 2011)

- If you are ever in a situation where the police want to question you, it is your legal right to demand that an attorney be present. It is the police officer's job to try to get you to answer questions. It is your job to ONLY say, "I would like an attorney." Then, wait until one arrives before saying anything more. (HCCAA 2011)

- Always talk respectfully to a police officer. Do not try to state your point of view repeatedly, as this could sound argumentative. (HCCAA 2010)

- If you have leftover prescription pain pills that you no longer need to take, know that it is illegal to sell them to anyone else even if someone asks to buy them from you. (HCCAA 2011)

- Sometimes at a big New Year's Eve party people kiss others on the lips at midnight, whether they know the person or not. This is probably the only time it is O.K. to kiss a total stranger. (HCCAA 2011)

- When using the self-scanner at a store checkout, if an item doesn't scan and you proceed to place it in your shopping bag as if it had scanned, this is considered stealing. (HCCAA 2011)

- Even if you think you are right, never argue with a police officer if you are pulled over when driving. (HCCAA 2011)

✳ **ACTIVITY:** Choose your favorite way to record important information such as on your iPad, computer, or a notebook and begin a list of illegal behaviors that you engage in that could get you arrested. (When adults engage in illegal behavior, they may or may not get arrested. The consequences of illegal behavior vary, typically according to the seriousness of the behavior.) You can ask trusted friends, relatives and social service people on your team (if you have such a team) to give you suggestions for your list. After you have several items on your list, you may further categorize them. For ideas on categories, keep reading. When you become aware of which behaviors are illegal, you are in a better position to avoid engaging in behaviors that could potentially get you into trouble with the police.

# Temple Grandin's Categories of Social Sins

Inhibiting social comments is very important if you are an autistic person, especially if you do not understand the hidden curriculum. Even though I had memorized many items from the illegal list above, my problem was in figuring out when to inhibit and when not to inhibit. I understood how very important this could be to avoid big trouble, but my *modus operandi* was to be very quiet in public so as to avoid mistakes unless I was with one of my very trusted friends.

My business was expanding and required more social contacts and traveling, so I needed to be able to figure this out
because more and more often I was not in the company of a
friend. It was no longer enough to merely avoid legal trouble.
I also wanted to avoid social embarrassment with new business contacts.

One strategy I employed was to learn all I could by reading
about other successful adult autistics. I learned a lot simply
from reading books written by adults on the autism spectrum,
including *Like Color to the Blind* (Williams, 1996), *Finding a
Different Kind of Normal* (Purkis, 2006), *Elijah's Cup* (Paradiz,
2002), *Pretending to Be Normal* (Willey, 1999) and *Thinking in
Pictures* (Grandin, 1995).

The interesting thing is that I had already read all these
books. In fact, they were on my bookshelves. But I had never
read them to intentionally glean information that would be
useful to me in learning hidden curriculum. In that way, all my
old books became new books to me. When I had first read
these books I did not have any hidden curriculum categories
in my head so I had not recorded any hidden curriculum information. That is, since these data had never been entered they
could not be retrieved. So, I reread these books and intentionally inserted data into my recently formed hidden curriculum categories so that I would be able to retrieve them at
some future time when the occasion presented itself.

I already knew it was most important not to commit a social sin that was illegal. My categories were never-do-illegal-stuff and after-the-fact-embarrassing-stuff. I discovered from Temple Grandin a very practical, even finer, sort on social sin categories (http://www.iidc.indiana.edu/index.php?pageId=600). This is the best explanation of this topic I have ever come across. Temple sorts social sins into four categories: courtesy rules, illegal but not bad, really bad things and sins of the system. This is how she explains these four categories.

## • Courtesy Rules

In Temple's categorization, these are the rules that demonstrate respect for your fellow human beings. Following them makes others feel more comfortable and keeps them from becoming mad at you. Here are some examples.

### Hidden Curriculum Items: Courtesy Rules

- Do not touch a pregnant woman's belly unless you have been invited to do so by the woman.

- In most cases, it is not appropriate to go up to another person and adjust the clothing he is wearing unless the person is your child, spouse or significant other.

- When finding a seat on a bus, it is expected that you will not sit next to a stranger if other seats are available.

- Even though it is a commonly understood social courtesy not to pick your nose in public places, it is not your place to inform a nose picker unless the nose picker is your child.

- It is important to inhibit the urge to touch other people's clothing even if you are attracted to the feel of the fabric or the look of a decoration, etc.

- Adults generally pick up after themselves, whether in their own home, the home of a friend or in a public place.

- When offered food, it is better to say, "No thanks" than to say, "I don't want to eat that food." Even though it may be true that you don't want to eat the food, that sort of remark is most often perceived as rude and hurtful.

- When invited to a party advertising hors d'oeuvres, it means there will be small portions, usually bite-sized pieces of food to nibble on during the party. It is not meant to be a full meal, so plan accordingly.

- When eating with friends or family, everyone generally waits until all are finished eating before leaving the table.

- When riding in a friend's car, it is considered impolite to reach over and change the radio station, even if you hate the music playing, unless you are specifically told that you can do so.

## • Illegal, But Not Bad

Technically, many things are illegal, but not necessarily bad. For example, Temple (http://www.iidc.indiana.edu/index. php?pageId=600) explains that speeding is illegal, but if one considers why the law about speeding exists – to prevent car accidents – it is easy to see that speeding a little bit when traffic is light and weather conditions are good is not bad even though technically it would be illegal. A person must be careful when breaking one of these rules because if caught, a punishment could result, such as, in this example, a speeding ticket. Here are a few examples of these sorts of sins.

## Hidden Curriculum Items: Illegal, But Not Bad

- Sometimes in a parking lot, cars are parked over the yellow line. Even though it may be irritating and it is a fact that a car is not meant to take up more than one parking space, it is generally not socially acceptable or necessary to report it to the police.

- If you walk your dog, it is important to know and obey the leash law in your community. Most communities have specific areas where dogs must be on a leash. Breaking this law can result in the owner being fined. (HCCAA 2011)

- Ordering pizza delivery to somebody's home as a prank is punishable by law. (HCCAA 2011)

- Pull over to the far-right side of the road and stop whenever there is a vehicle with a siren on the road. Once the vehicle has passed, you may resume your travels. (HCCAA 2011)

- Call 911 only for life-threatening or potentially life-threatening emergencies such as a car accident or a robbery under-way. Finding a stray animal or having noisy children playing in the neighborhood may feel like an emergency, but they are not life-threatening events. (HCCAA 2011)

- If you come to a stop too closely behind a school bus equipped with an automatic camera that takes pictures of vehicles that come too close, you can expect to receive a ticket in the mail.

- While it is considered jaywalking to cross the street in the middle of the block, many people do so. Unless you are a police officer, it is not your business to comment on or to scold a jaywalker. (HCCAA 2010)

- Most communities have time frames for how long before and after trash pickup you can leave your trash can at the curb. You may be fined if you put your trash out too early or leave it out too long after the trash has been picked up. (HCCAA 2010)

## • Really Bad Things

These are behaviors that are highly destructive or physically harmful. They are against the law and will be punished. They are things like murder, arson, rape, lying under oath, stealing, looting and injuring other people. Most of the items that I placed in my illegal list above would go in Temple's (http://www.iidc.indiana.edu/index.php?pageId=600) category of Really Bad Things.

## • Sins of the System (SOS)

These so-called sins are so severe that one must never break them – whether or not they make sense – because the penalty is severe. They vary from culture to culture and from country to country. In the United States, two SOSs are sexual misbehavior and drug offenses. It is important to know the SOSs because you must never ever do them.

Both Temple and I have decided to simply inform ourselves and then memorize the lists because, whether we understand any of the nuances or not, the results of committing any of these sins is so severe that we don't want to take the chance. Temple has decided this for her category of Sins of the System (http://www.iidc.indiana.edu/index.php?pageId=600). I have decided this for my category above called illegal list.

**ACTIVITY:** Using the items from the Illegal list, Courtesy Rules and Illegal, But Not Bad, sort the items into categories that make sense for you. Name your categories. Make sure you have a category of sins that you know to avoid at all costs due to the legal ramifications of committing them. If you have started recording a list of your own illegal behaviors (see previous Activity), you can also categorize items from that list.

## Categories of Variables

It was very helpful to me to read *The Hidden Curriculum: Practical Solutions for Understanding Unstated Rules in Social Situations* (Myles et al., 2004). Especially helpful was learning some of the variables related to the hidden curriculum.

One of these variables that nobody ever explains to you as you grow up is that **lots of rules change**. For example, it is perfectly fine for a kindergartener to hold his mother's hand when walking into school, but if a fifth grader did this, he would become a target for teasing and, possibly, bullying.

The hand-holding rule changes again when we grow up. Once you are old enough to date, hand holding becomes a romantic gesture, and still later it becomes a helpful gesture as parents become aged and physically need the assistance of a hand to navigate some public settings.

Reading through the list of hidden curriculum variables and examples of each helped me a lot in terms of having structure of another way to sort out and think about the hidden curriculum. I needed this visual word "structure" in my head so I could pop it up and have a place to record the hidden curriculum items I observed.

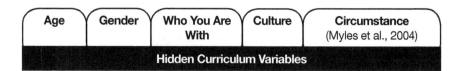

| Age | Gender | Who You Are With | Culture | Circumstance (Myles et al., 2004) |
|-----|--------|------------------|---------|-----------------------------------|
| **Hidden Curriculum Variables** | | | | |

Once this word outline was created, it served as a visual I could pop up in my head when I needed a place to record information. It wasn't that I was observing new information, but I now had a way to record and store it. This was great because not all items fit into Temple's (http://www.iidc.indiana.edu/index.php?pageId=600) hierarchy of social sin construct; I needed more categories. After I had these categories of hidden curriculum variables, I could incorporate what I saw in the world around me in a way that made sense and that I was able to retrieve later. This became much more efficient for me than trying to keep track of the thousands of individual hidden curriculum items I had accumulated.

My brain doesn't seem to automatically categorize information, but I found that these categories made a positive difference. First, I manually input items I observed into the correct category on my list. After several months of doing this, one day I discovered items in the categories that I knew I had not manually put there. Somehow my brain had automatically put the new item into the correct category without me being aware of it!

Even though I still wasn't learning the hidden curriculum ahead of committing social sins, I was happy that I could now look at others and learn from their sins rather than needing to sin myself in order to categorize and store hidden curriculum items for future reference. This is what I hope this book will do for others.

## • Age-Related Variables

It is important for adults with autism spectrum disorders to learn the hidden curriculum that changes with age. Not understanding age-related variables can be more damaging than social embarrassment. As we saw earlier, sometimes behavior that a child can get by with can incur legal consequences for an adult displaying the same behavior.

The following list illustrates age-related variables of the hidden curriculum. (Please note there are age-related items in some of the previous lists, such as the illegal, that may also be put into this section.)

### Hidden Curriculum Items: Age-Related Variables

- It is common for children to tell their age to new friends. This is not information that adults usually share when meeting new friends. (HCCAA, 2010)

- Age ranges on toys and games are guidelines meant to advertise that most often children of the stated age range will enjoy a given toy or game. It is perfectly fine for anyone, including you, to enjoy the toy or game even if you do not fall into the specified age range. (HCCAA, 2010)

- When choosing a gift for a child, it is important not to get something that is below the child's age range. Most children will classify such a gift as a "baby toy" and often will have nothing to do with it. (HCCAA, 2010)

- When playing a game with a young child, it is better to let the child win than to end up with a crying child who lost, even if you are the better player. (HCCAA, 2010)

- Once you become an adult, you typically receive fewer presents for your birthday and for Christmas than you received as a child. This does not mean that people care less about you.

- A gift of roses or candy on Valentine's Day is most often interpreted as an expression of romantic interest. (HCCAA, 2010)

- If it is a custom in your family to pull the wishbone from the Thanksgiving turkey, even if you have done this for many years, know that you will likely be expected to graciously give up your spot to any child who may be present. (HCCAA, 2010)

- Even though you may have loved the custom of trick-or-treating as a child, you are no longer able to do this as an adult. But sometimes adults have Halloween parties where the guests dress in costumes. (HCCAA, 2011)

- Even though as a small child you may have enjoyed sitting on Santa's lap at the mall, it is not something you may do as an adult. The exception would be at a special party where sitting on Santa's lap is O.K. for anyone to do, including adults. (HCCAA, 2011)

- Sometimes a child has a napkin tucked under his chin to act as a bib. It is usually not acceptable for an adult to do so. (HCCAA, 2010)

## • Gender-Related Variables

Another important hidden curriculum variable to learn is gender differences. I am a person who happens to believe in gender equality. Gender-based hidden curriculum variables have nothing to do with gender equality; it is about the prevailing socially accepted gender roles. Take, for example, the simple act of using a public restroom. Men typically do not employ

this as a social occasion for conversation while women often do. In fact, women at a social function typically go to the
restroom in pairs or groups, often for the express purpose of
yacking it up with one another. If you are a woman it is fine to
be friendly in a public restroom. But if you are a man and start
yacking it up in a public restroom, totally different assumptions
are made about you, such as you are gay or mentally ill (Myles
at al., 2004).  Based on these assumptions, you could unwit-
tingly become a target for sexual assault.

This is but one example of gender differences, but you can probably begin to see why it is important that autistics, who don't
generally automatically pick up hidden curriculum information, are
either directly taught or find a way to learn the gender-based hidden curriculum. Not knowing and following the hidden curriculum
for your gender has varying degrees of repercussions.

**ACTIVITY:** As you read through the following examples,
try to imagine what might happen if you did not know this
information or did not follow the hidden curriculum for
your gender.  Pick a few examples and draw out a car-
toon, talk about it with a trusted friend, or write a short
story of something that might happen as a result of not
following one of these hidden curriculum items.

## Hidden Curriculum Items: Gender-Related Variables

- When a guy refers to a gal as "easy," he means that she is sexually accessible without a lot of persuasion.

- Even though it is referred to as cleavage when clothing reveals the crack between women's breasts, it is improper to refer to the crack revealed when men's pants hang too low as cleavage. In fact, it is best not to talk about it.

- When someone is said to have "been around," it means they have had intimate relationships with others. There is a gender difference in the social assumptions applied to this behavior, meaning it is often considered O.K. for guys (he's a stud!) but not O.K. for gals (she's a slut!).

- If you are a middle-aged woman and experience physiological power surges that produce excessive body heat, it is likely a hot flash. Hot flashes are normal. If they become too uncomfortable, consult your physician. (HCCAA, 2010)

- Women who know each other often talk to one another in public restrooms; men rarely talk to other men in restrooms even if they know them. Act according to your gender. (HCCAA, 2010)

## • Who-You-Are-With Variables

It can be hard to learn the hidden curriculum because so many hidden rules are subject to exceptions. Sometimes a behavior that is perfectly fine in the presence of one person is considered socially wrong when in the company of another person.

For example, one of my friends considers it rude for visitors to her home to take off their shoes. At another friend's home, it is customary for everyone to remove their shoes at the door. In fact, there is a special mat at both the front and the back door where shoes are supposed to be left before entering the house. These mats are usually full of several pairs of shoes. Every

weekend the children in this family must put
all their shoes from the mats back into their
closets to get ready for the weekend
housecleaning to happen. When I go to
visit at the home of friends, whether I take
off or leave on my shoes totally depends on
which friend's home I am
visiting.

Here are some hidden curriculum
items illustrating the who-you-are-with variable, which, of
course, goes way beyond shoes.

## Hidden Curriculum Items: Who-You-Are-With Variables

- Sometimes workers in places such as fast food restaurants or banks wear red Christmas hats as a way to look festive. No matter how ridiculous you might think they look, it is best to keep it to yourself.

- When visiting a friend, do not help yourself to anything in the refrigerator or cupboards unless you have been invited to do so or have asked and received permission.

- If a date asks, "Do you want some action?" it could be a reference to intimacy depending upon the context of the situation.

- Even though most people would agree that gossiping is wrong, most people engage in it to some extent. When gossiping, it is important to only do so with a very few very trusted close friends.

- It is inconsiderate to volunteer your friends to do something you are unable to do without first checking with them.

- Even though your doctor and other medical workers ask you personal questions, you may not ask the same questions of them. (HCCAA, 2010)

- Sometimes your friend will not want you to repeat what she told you to another person, and at other times your friend will not care if you do so. If in doubt, ask your friend before you repeat what she has told you. (HCCAA, 2010)

- While it's good to arrive a bit early for appointments, it's often considered rude to arrive early to people's homes for social functions. (HCCAA, 2010)

- While it is fine to give your nieces and nephews monetary gifts for their birthdays, it is usually better to give your parents and other adult relatives a wrapped gift. (HCCAA, 2010)

- When phoning people, it is generally considered good etiquette to avoid calling early in the morning or after 9 o'clock at night. (HCCAA, 2010)

## • Culture-Related Variables

Culture can be thought of as the ideas and values of a group of people. Countries, religions, and even families, have their own cultures. Sometimes groups of people (such as those who have autism spectrum disorder, those who are on a sports team, those who are employed at a particular workplace, etc.) develop shared values, hold certain ideas in high esteem and employ particular behaviors. In this way, these kinds of groups can be thought of as having their own culture.

Each cultural grouping, besides having shared ideas and values, also have a shared hidden curriculum. An example is the idea that burping loudly after a meal is considered rude in most cultures, but in some cultures this behavior is considered to be a compliment to the cook.

## Hidden Curriculum Items: Culture-Related Variables

- When people celebrate different holidays than you do, it shows polite interest to ask about their holiday and customs. In addition, these facts are often interesting to learn about. (HCCAA, 2011)

- In places of worship, do not take money out of the offering basket even if your intent is to make change for your contribution. (HCCAA, 2010)

- There is no need to talk loudly to a person using a wheelchair or a walker unless he or she also has a hearing problem.

- Don't blow out candles inside churches or other place of worship. They often have religious significance and it is not up to a guest in the church to blow them out.

- When a visitor to a place of worship, it is best to watch and try to fit in whether or not you understand what is going on. Afterwards you may ask the friend or relative who invited you about a custom you are interested in learning.

- Japanese food isn't only for Japanese people. It is perfectly fine to eat Japanese (or any ethnic) food regardless of your race or ethnicity.

- In some families, each person makes a holiday or birthday wish list. Even though it may be the most efficient way to ensure receiving a desired gift, do not give your friends a gift list unless they ask for one. (HCCAA, 2010)

- RSVP stated on an invitation is a French phrase that translates to mean "please respond." It is standard practice to reply to an RSVP request whether confirming attendance or declining. (HCCAA, 2010)

- When having a conversation, keep in mind the general rule that each person talks approximately the same amount of time. Be sure to talk some, but be careful not to talk more than others. (HCCAA, 2011)

- Each person uses his free time in a way that is enjoyable to him. It is a personal choice. It is inappropriate to tell someone how to spend his free time. (HCCAA, 2010)

## • Circumstance-Related Variables

The most difficult hidden curriculum variable for me to learn has to do with the fact that **the hidden curriculum rules change as circumstances change**. First of all, it is usually difficult for me to realize when circumstances have changed. This in and of itself makes it extraordinarily difficult to then know whether the hidden rules I have learned for a particular circumstance apply.

An example is when I visit my friend Anika. Her house feels to me like my own home. I do all the things, such as cook, wash clothes, load the dishwasher, etc., that I do at my own house. With another friend, Vanessa, I also carry on in a very relaxed manner, but because she has an adult son and a husband living at her house, I do not go around in my pajamas as I might at Anika's house. When I visited yet another friend, Carly, I was fully dressed, with my hair brushed, etc., at all times and never would think to take stuff out of her refrigerator like I would at Anika's house or open her cupboard to get a glass for a drink of water like I would do at both Anika's and at Vanessa's house.

Being a guest in the homes of Anika, Vanessa and Carly represents three totally different sets of circumstances with different expectations for how I am to behave. So, even though I am a guest and visiting friends, the circumstances are different in the homes of each of these friends. This results in a different hidden curriculum in each situation.

The following list illustrates the hidden curriculum that is based on circumstances. In each case there is a general rule – sometimes stated and at other times merely assumed. Then, because of the changing circumstance, an exception to the rule is made.

## Hidden Curriculum Items: Circumstance-Related Variables

- People generally do not contact their friends who are on vacation except in the case of an emergency. An exception would be when different arrangements have been made ahead of time.

- On St. Patrick's Day it is customary for places serving beer to color it green. This does not affect the taste or alcohol content of the beer, only the color.

- If you are a person who notices the smell of a house when you walk in, know that it is generally O.K. to comment positively on a smell such as pie baking in the oven or a scented candle, but making a negative comment, such as the smell of a cat litter box or garbage, is considered rude.

- Some sporting events have half time. Theater events have intermission. Both are breaks midway through the event.

- If you see your doctor in a public place such as the post office or the grocery store, simply issue a friendly greeting. Do not talk about any of your medical concerns.

- At a movie theater, your ticket is good for any seat in the theater. At a performing arts theater, your ticket is generally good for a specific seat, so you must sit in that seat.

- In movie theaters, it is considered a common courtesy not to sit down next to a stranger. However, if the theater is crowded, it is fine to do so.

- Sometimes weather conditions are such that it is unsafe to drive the speed limit. In fact, if driving the speed limit is deemed unsafe for road conditions, a police officer can issue a ticket to a driver who is traveling at the posted speed.

- When you are shopping in a store, you are expected to pay the price listed on the item you are purchasing. When you are shopping for a car, you are expected to offer to pay a lower price than the price listed on the car. The final price is then negotiated with the salesperson. (HCCAA, 2010)

- Teenagers almost always whisper and laugh together in the library. If this bothers you, move to another part of the library. You do not need to say anything to the teens or report it to the librarian. (HCCAA, 2010)

★ **ACTIVITY:** Think of situations when you were surprised to discover an already learned hidden curriculum item didn't work so well in a new circumstance. Write down the general hidden curriculum rule along with the exception. Here is an example:

*General Rule:* It is a courtesy rule not to make noise in the neighborhood early in the morning.

*Exception:* It is O.K. to use a snow blower early in the morning if you need to get your car out after an overnight snowfall.

## Chapter Three:

# Figuring out Proactive Strategies to Cut Down on Social Embarrassment

Because I had made the decision to keep on trying to learn the hidden curriculum and because of the feeling of embarrassment that came after seeing others' negative reactions to my behavior, I decided to figure out how to cut down on my embarrassment. In a way, it was a matter of survival. I needed to not feel so bad about myself on a continual basis. I still had hopes of cracking the code – of figuring out the hidden curriculum before making social blunders – but it became increasingly clear that I wasn't going to learn this any time soon. Therefore, in the meantime, I needed to cut down on my own feelings of embarrassment. This continues to be necessary in terms of my personal comfort, my professional life and my quest to continue learning all I can in order to fit more comfortably into the world around me.

Following are the proactive strategies I have found helpful in terms of avoiding embarrassing social mistakes.

# Pause and Match

A difficulty I come up against time after time is that, because of my autism, my brain automatically tries to pull up a literal interpretation of things I hear in conversation. So, without even giving it a thought, my brain automatically runs the words I hear people say though this literal filter. Often I would respond to my literal understanding of what people said and then, after the fact, find out that my response was inappropriate.

For example, once a friend asked if I knew how to get to a coffee shop on the other side of town. I replied that I did and then went on to talk about something else. Finally, she asked if I was going to give her the directions or if she needed to look them up on MapQuest. Her comment made me feel stupid and embarrassed. It made sense that she had asked if I knew the directions because she needed them and wanted me to give them to her, not just to check on whether I know them or not, which would have served no functional purpose in the context.

Later, on my drive home, I was thinking about this and realized that many times I wind up embarrassed because I respond out of my autistic, literal style of thinking. I don't decide to do it or even think about it. It automatically happens. One of my natural ways of making sense out of language is through this literal filter.

What if I merely paused before responding to people? Would a momentary pause allow me the time to figure out if my literal response matched the intent of the question or the conversation?

I had nothing to lose by testing this. So, I did. In the beginning, I found that I could do it sometimes, but not always. Then, the more I had opportunity to practice, the better I became at my pause-and-match strategy.

Over time, I learned that just because I seem to be wired to first interpret language literally didn't mean I could not retrain myself to look beyond this first interpretation. This is especially important when the first interpretation doesn't make a whole lot of sense.

### • Sayings That Do Not Literally Mean What They Say

Often the first meaning I learned for a word became my literal interpretation of that word, which made it hard to understand when these words were used differently. But I found that if I used my pause-and-match technique, it worked well for this.

If something doesn't make sense, I pause and ask myself: Is there another meaning? Sometimes when I can't figure it out, I ask a trusted friend. If a friend is not available just then, I do my best. For example, the first time I traveled on an international flight alone, the saying "please swipe passport" at the check-in kiosk didn't make sense to me. My literal picture for "swipe" was a pickpocket situation where a man in black jeans and t-shirt swipes a wallet from another man's pocket. As a result, I thought the instruction "please swipe passport" was instructing me to steal a fellow passenger's passport!

Because of my personal quest to learn the hidden curriculum, I knew enough to check this initial interpretation and pause and match. After pausing, I could still not figure out the intent of the instruction and, therefore, could not match my response to the intent. I also knew I could get in big legal trouble if I acted on my literal interpretation of the kiosk instruction, which, by the way, did not make a whole lot of sense.

With no friends around to ask in the moment, I announced, "I'm really sorry, but I cannot do this." Even though I was referring to not stealing a fellow passenger's passport, the airline agent assumed I meant that I was having trouble following the kiosk self-check-in instructions. He promptly came over to help, took my passport from my hand and "swiped" it. Once I saw him do that, I was able to immediately switch my picture/thought of the pickpocket to swiping my credit card at the grocery checkout.

Because it is often difficult for my brain to make a quick switch, even though I know an alternative meaning for a word such as "swipe" actually exists, I am not always able to access that information just when I need it. Thus, the pause-and-match rule has "saved" me numerous times. The following list illustrates several examples.

## Hidden Curriculum Items: Sayings That Do Not Literally Mean What They Say

- "Brainwashed" has nothing to do with the cleanliness of your brain. It is a term used to mean that you have been convinced of something due to another person using tricky tactics that lead you believe something you would normally not believe.

- The expression "my peeps" is a way of talking about one's group of friends. It has nothing to do with a person, sometimes referred to as a peeping Tom, who secretly peers at another who isn't aware of it.

- When someone you are talking to on the phone says, "I need to let you go," they are indicating they would like to end the phone conversation. It is considerate to wind up your conversation and say goodbye in a few moments.

- If someone says, "Don't stick your nose where it doesn't belong," they are politely telling you to stop asking questions or talking about something they consider none of your business. It is best to say you are sorry and change the subject.

- "Early-bird special" has nothing to do with chicken cooked earlier in the day. It refers to a restaurant meal served at discount prices prior the restaurant's busiest hours.

- If someone becomes a "laughing stock," they did something so stupid or wrong that no one can take them seriously, and people scorn and/or laugh at them.

- "Unisex" does not mean a person is both male and female. It is a term used to signify that use by both males and females is acceptable. This can apply to restrooms, clothing, bicycles, etc.

- Saying a person has sticky fingers is an accusation of theft.

- The phrase "let it snow" is a general comment about snow falling rather than granting permission for it to snow. Snowfall is a weather phenomenon that happens when conditions are right whether you would like it or not.

- The phrase "on the other hand" is used to signify that what is to follow is another, often opposing, consideration or point of view.

- If something is referred to as a "sacred cow," it likely has nothing to do with Hinduism. Something that is a sacred cow is held in such respect that you are meant to not criticize or suggest it be changed.

- When elderly people talk about being "bound up," it has nothing to do with being tied up with ropes. Being bound up is a reference to being constipated.

- The saying "suck it up" has nothing to do with drinking through a straw. It means to do your best accepting a situation that cannot be changed without complaining.

## • Idioms

When I use the pause-and-match strategy, it catches a lot of idioms. As an autistic person, I often have a hard time initially understanding idioms, but even so, idioms can be learned. The interesting thing for me is that even though I have learned the meanings of many idioms over the years, my brain still tends to automatically interpret the words of an idiom in a literal manner.

For example, when I hear, "Haste makes waste," my automatic understanding involves a picture of a garbage can popping up in my head – the waste part. Then, I see myself running my garbage can down to the end of my driveway as quickly as I can in readiness for trash pick-up day. However, with my pause-and-match technique, I now pause and realize that running my garbage can down to the end of my driveway does not match the intent of the person who said, "Haste makes waste." The pause is all that is necessary, because I know that "haste makes waste" is an idiom and had long ago learned its meaning. It just isn't my automatic first interpretation of the words used in creating that idiom.

Here is a list of idioms and other sayings that I totally understand, but for which conventional understanding is rarely the first interpretation that is automatically applied by my literal brain.

## Hidden Curriculum Items: List of Idioms

- To "hit the books" means to spend time in concentrated study. Students often say this when they need to study for exams.

- To "face the music" means that you accept any unpleasant consequences of your actions or behavior.

- When it is said that a person is looking at you through green eyes, it means the person is envious of you; "green" has to do with envy rather than eye color.

- When a woman says she has "a bun in the oven," it means she is pregnant. It has nothing to do with baking.

- Even though it may sound like it, the phrase "bangers and mash" is not an idiom. Bangers and mash is a common reference to a meal of sausage and potatoes. In fact, it can be found on the breakfast menu of restaurants in many countries, but especially in British-influenced countries.

- A glutton is a person who eats a lot. A "glutton for punishment" is an idiom meaning a person happily accepts jobs or tasks most people would try to get out of.

- When someone asks if she can "bend your ear," she is asking if you will listen to her while she talks through a problem or situation.

- If someone says they "feel like death warmed over," it means they feel exhausted or sick. It does not mean they are sick enough to actually die. In fact, this saying has nothing to do with death.

- When someone says he "saved his skin," it means he avoided getting into trouble.

- Something that is poorly thought out and can easily collapse or fail is sometimes referred to as "a house of cards."

# Laugh Along

All my life I have mixed up words that sound alike but have very different meanings. For example, I was once introduced as a "prolific" writer (very much stretching the truth, I think, but it is what was said). I later announced to another friend that I had been called a "prophylactic" writer. Interchanging sound alike words like this doesn't usually work well!

Even though this can be funny at times, it is hard to get others to take you seriously after making such word mix-up blunders. Often, you wind up sounding like a fool. This can negatively effect employment, friendships and pretty much life in general.

Initially I tried to apply the pause-and-match strategy to see if I could avoid word mix-ups. That didn't work. Because I was the person generating the words, it meant that I had to think through and consider each spoken sentence before speaking it. Needless to say, this is impossible to do and still remain part of any sort of conversation. So it quickly became evident that I would need a different strategy.

Most of the time, I don't realize when I have used a sound-alike word that means something totally different than what was intended. Sometimes the different word is close enough so that it doesn't matter, but at other times it does matter. If somebody starts laughing, I immediately laugh along. Most times I don't understand why I am laughing. Luckily, it usually doesn't matter because most people like to laugh with you. Funny thing is that the other person usually makes enough of a comment that I come to understand why we are both laughing. If not, I can usually figure it out later, or if I trust the person enough I can let him or her in on the secret that I don't have a clue why we are laughing. Then, once the situation has been explained, we both have a really good laugh together!

Based on personal experience here are some important word mix-ups to avoid. If you also make them, be sure to laugh along!

## Hidden Curriculum Word Mix-Ups

- "House guest" and "house pet" sound similar, but have quite different meanings. Be careful not to mix them up, especially when referring to overnight company.

- In the texting world, LOL does not mean Lots of Love. It means Laugh out Loud. Therefore, it would be inappropriate to send messages such as, "Sorry about your accident, LOL." (HCCAA, 2011)

- "Filtration" and "flirtation" are similar words with different meanings. "Filtration" is a process of making water clean. "Flirtation" is coy behavior meant to attract a potential romantic interest.

- The term "hooking up" has multiple meanings having to do with connecting people. Some people use the term to indicate connecting two people in a business or social realm. Others use it to mean that they had sex, such as "I hooked up with Susan last night."

- Being a glutton for punishment has nothing to do with eating a food you shouldn't eat because you are allergic to gluten.

- All adults have gone through puberty, but not adultery. "Puberty" is the stage of growth and development where reproduction becomes physiologically possible. "Adultery" is when a married person cheats on a spouse.

- "Putting a baby to sleep" involves a bedtime routine such as feeding or rocking until the baby falls asleep. "Putting a pet to sleep" means having the pet euthanized, usually by a vet.

- "Peep shows" refer to adult entertainment where a person looks through a small hole or magnifying glass to see X-rated pictures that often include nudity and sex. Peep shows have nothing to do with the yellow marshmallow treats called Peeps. (HCCAA, 2010)

- Even though strong trash bags are often labeled "hefty," it is not a compliment to use this word to describe a strong person. For example, don't call the nurse who pumps up the blood pressure cuff a hefty pumper. "Hefty" in reference to a person means fat rather than strong. (HCCAA, 2010)

# Recognize and Expand Black-and-White Thinking

In addition to a literal way of thinking, I also tend to have a very black-and-white manner of thinking. Things are either absolutely one way or absolutely the opposite way. It has been difficult for me to understand the shades of grey in the middle. In this way of thinking, if things are not right, they are wrong; not hot then cold; not happy then sad – and that's that!

Take for example the truth vs. lie dichotomy. For most of my life, if something wasn't the absolute truth, by default, it was a lie to me. One day a friend and colleague, Lysa, who was in graduate school, told me she would be happy to get a "B" in a class she was taking. Because I knew she was a high achiever and had never been happy with anything less than an "A" grade, I told her she was lying.

In the ensuing discussion Lysa reframed her lie into a "wishing truth." She said that because the class was so difficult, she was trying to wish herself to be happy with a "B" grade. Thus, she wasn't lying but stating a wishing truth.

To help myself incorporate the concept of shades of grey into my black-and-white thinking, I made a horizontal visual. On the far right side is a black box and on the far left side a white box. In the space between the black and the white boxes is a swatch of color fading from black into white, which produces numerous shades of grey (see page 57).

## Chapter Three: Figuring out Proactive Strategies to Cut Down on Social Embarrassment

Because I am a visual thinker, this visual allowed me a way to expand my black-and-white thinking by providing a spot for me to slide various lies I encountered. The grays allowed me to see that not all lies were of the same intensity. It made it easier to understand that many so-called lies fall into this grey area. Because the grey area is made up of both black and white color, I could see that I was identifying with the black part of the grey while Lysa was identifying with the white part of the grey. This resulted in me believing Lysa was telling a lie whereas Lysa believed she was telling a "wishing truth." Seeing the grey area in my visual allowed me to literally *see* that Lysa and I were at the same grey spot in our understanding, but that each of us was perceiving it a bit differently – me seeing the blackness of the grey and Lysa seeing the whiteness of the same grey.

Even though I think of this as Lysa saying sliding-scale lies, I also have come to understand that much of what I consider a lie is on this sliding scale and that most of the population views many of these "grey lies" as variations of truth. Using this visual allowed me to expand my black-and-white thinking in a way that made sense to me and allowed me to understand the way others thought about things. I could see that often we thought the same way, even when we were using absolute dichotomous words that had opposite meanings to describe our understanding of a circumstance. The following list of hidden curriculum items illustrates aspects of black-and-white thinking.

## Hidden Curriculum Items: Black-and-White Thinking

- Even though people may ask to "borrow" a tissue, they do not intend to return it to you after they use it.

- Even though it is a fact that a person's home is messy, do not say so. This sort of comment is perceived by most people to be hurtful.

- It is considered rude to tell someone you don't like her enough to be her friend, even if it is true. There is nothing to be gained by sharing such information. Doing so only hurts others' feelings.

- One sort of music isn't better than another. Each person has his own likes and dislikes when it comes to music. It is perfectly fine to be friends with someone whose personal taste in music does not match yours.

- Regardless of your own belief, it is considerate to go along with a child's belief in Santa Claus as that is how the child understands the spirit of Christmas giving. The child is not wrong even if he believes differently than you.

- Even though you may think it is gross to have the presidents on the bills in your wallet facing each other as if to kiss, others will likely not even give it a thought. It is not something people generally talk about.

- At museums, generally, there is no set amount of time you are meant to look at each display. Patrons are free to look at displays for any length of time they wish during the hours the museum is open.

- Sometimes at an amusement park, a parent will wait in a long line, and when he is close to the front of the line his children will join him. Though this can be irksome, it is not considered butting in line and is permissible.

- Your way of preparing food is a personal preference. There are generally many ways to prepare the same dish. When others do it differently than you, they are not doing it wrong.

- Setting out a mousetrap is more than simply setting a new, packaged mousetrap on the floor in a corner. It also means to make the trap ready to catch a mouse. To do this, follow the directions that come with the mousetrap.

- You may think your brand of computer or cell phone is the best, but this is merely your opinion. Believing your opinion to be the truth does not make it a fact.

- Sometimes a person says, "You can't just take it without asking first." This implies you will get a "yes" answer after asking. If the answer is "no," then you cannot take the item even though you have asked first. A "yes" answer signifies permission to take the item you asked for.

- Even though it is true, if you don't want to talk on the phone it would be better not to answer it than to answer it and say, "I don't want to talk to you."

★**ACTIVITY:** Make your own shades of grey visual. Draw three squares with sides touching so they are in a line. Make the first square white, the second grey and the third black to look like this:

Now use an example from your own life to write in the squares. Here is an example from my life.

# Effective Perspective Taking

As an autistic, it doesn't work well for me to try to follow the admonition "put yourself in someone else's shoes," suggesting that if I do that I will somehow magically wind up understanding exactly how this other person thinks and feels. It seems to me this involves a multistep process.

First of all, to "put myself in someone else's shoes" means I am supposed to think about how I would feel if I were in the same circumstance.

Second, it is assumed that once I think this through, I will have a similar feeling to the neurotypical (NT) person.

Third, it is thought that I will be able to act, based on my now similar feeling, in a way that will be much appreciated by the NT experiencing a given circumstance or difficulty.

Looking at these three steps, I am very able to accomplish Step One. I can think about how I would feel if I were in the same circumstance. Step Two is where the problem comes in, because very often if I were in the same circumstance, because of my autistic thinking style, I would not wind up feeling the same way an NT person feels. Then, when looking at the third step, yes, I am able to act on my feelings, but it won't work out well socially for me because my feelings likely will not match the feelings of the NT.

Take for example the time I left the home of a friend without saying good-bye. We were done visiting, so I left. Later, I found out my friend's feelings were hurt because I hadn't said good-bye; she wondered what she had said or done to deserve what she considered rude treatment. She guessed that she had somehow offended me.

None of this was true for me. I had simply left when the visit was over! No matter how much I think on this, I will never arrive at the same feelings as my friend. Thus, it will be of no benefit for me to try to put myself in her shoes. However, I can come to understand how my friend thinks and feels about this and then respond based on her take of the situation rather than on my take of it.

For most of my life, people have assumed that I am lacking because I have been unable to take their perspective. The truth is I can come to understand others' perspective and act on this understanding even though I do not naturally take their perspective. As an autistic, it is not necessary for me to take the perspective of NTs – I only need to understand their perspective to be able to act in a way that is socially desirable.

This isn't rocket science! The ways of the majority is assumed to be "right" and becomes a societal standard. Anyone who doesn't measure up to the standard is assumed to be deviant or "wrong." I don't believe most people even think about this. They are not trying to be mean or in any way think or behave badly to autistics. Instead, it is merely an assumption most people act on without giving it any, or very little, thought.

As an autistic, I have learned that when I understand the "majority-is-right" assumption, I can make the necessary accommodations to fit more comfortably into the NT world around me. In fact, I am an expert at making accommodations! I have been making successful accommodations for NTs all my life. I just haven't announced it or gotten credit for it.

For example, conventional social greetings do not come naturally to me. They simply make no sense from my perspective. I see no reason to speak words such as "Hello. How are you?" when it has already been socially decided that regardless of the facts of a person's life or circumstances, the answer to this general social greeting is, "Fine. How are you?" But because I know this social greeting is important to most NTs and because the world is largely populated by NTs, I use it so as to fit in. Even so, I do not make reference to the accommodation I am making for my NT friends each time I make the accommodation. I doubt people even realize I make this accommodation for them nearly every time we meet.

## • Learn How an NT Thinks
Rather than trying so hard to take someone else's perspective – when that perspective is very foreign to me – instead I try to understand the thinking style of an NT. In addition, I try to understand the way the feelings of NTs are attached to their

thinking because it is often different from mine and has to be accommodated for in order for me to fit more comfortably into the world around me.

To do this, I think of the NT and myself as characters in a play. This enables me to understand how to act in a compassionate manner based on someone else's perspective without having to figure out how to take that perspective as my own – something I am not able to do simply because my brain does not seem to work in the same manner as the brains of NTs.

Here are some examples of situations where I discovered it was important for me to learn the NT perspective:

---

## Hidden Curriculum Items: When Perspective Matters

- Though it is perfectly fine to like some friends better than others, it is not O.K. to tell your friends your preferences in this regard.

- Your driver's license may literally be lost. However, if you say, "I lost my license," the meaning people generally apply to this statement is that your driver's license has been legally taken away as a result of repeated traffic offenses.

- It is important to rake and dispose of the leaves in your yard in the same way others in your neighborhood do. If all your neighbors rake their leaves and you don't, you could be considered a bad neighbor.

- If you see an overweight person exercising, it will not be perceived as encouragement to tell him, "Good for you to be exercising. You really need it!"

- If you are entertaining yourself on a long plane, train or bus ride with a sound-emitting device such as an iPod or laptop, it is best to use headphones as other passengers often find this kind of sound annoying.

---

- Even if you know and can easily calculate how many calories are in food items on somebody's plate at a party, this is not the kind of information others appreciate you telling them. Keep it to yourself.

- At the conclusion of a visit with a friend, it is better to say, "goodbye" than to say, "I'm done with you now." For some unknown reason, even though it is true, most people feel offended by this remark.

- When choosing gifts, it is best to choose something the recipient will enjoy even if it is not something you would enjoy. (HCCAA, 2010)

- The number of gifts you receive for Christmas is not a measure of your personal value. Thus, if you receive more (or fewer) gifts this year than last year, it does not mean you are worth more (or less) to other people than you were the previous year.

- It is good manners to thank people when they give you gifts. If you do not feel thankful for the gift itself, don't mention it at all, but instead simply thank the giver for being thoughtful.

## • Play It Forward

I understand that thinking elicits feelings. I also understand that most NTs think in similar ways and that this, in turn, leads to shared feelings. However, because I don't always share this experience, I have had to figure it out another way. I can't understand by simply putting myself in others' shoes because even though I could and did put myself in their shoes, my neurology would not allow me to arrive at the same conclusion of a shared feeling.

Instead, I have learned to fast-forward the play (current life situation) so I can see in my head the various ways people might come to look as the scene plays out. I can work out the effects of various words and actions on the characters in the play I had running in my head. Fast-forwarding allows me to act in a way considered "appropriate" without having to understand why the characters would feel, and thus act, in the manner they did.

The amazing thing is that after I begin to act in a way that would make the scene come out favorably, the easier it was to pull it up again at a future time. In addition, after I had acted "correctly" several times, I could anticipate the feelings of others, and it was this anticipation that allowed me a soft feeling of my own – of wanting to relate to and be a part of making the scene come out nicely for all concerned.

Here is a list of items that I was able to guess by using my play-it-forward technique.

---

## Hidden Curriculum Items: Play It Forward

- If a sitcom character displays a negative attribute, it is not a good thing to tell your friend she reminds you of that character even if you mean it in a positive, complimentary way. (HCCAA, 2011)

- If people roll their eyes when you are speaking, it likely means that they think something is not quite right with what you are talking about or how you are expressing yourself. Also, it could mean they think what you are saying is boring. If that happens, it's a good idea to finish your sentence and stop talking. (HCCAA, 2010)

- When someone says, "It's nice to finally meet you in person," it is not good to respond, "I imagine that's quite true." Even though your intention is to be agreeable, most people would interpret that as a conceited remark.

- It is perfectly O.K. to rank your friends from best to worst, but don't share it with anyone. (HCCAA, 2011)

---

- If your friend says, "I'm such a klutz!" after having done something clumsy, it is considered impolite to agree, saying, "You sure are!" Even though she knows she is a klutz, as suggested by her comment, in most cases she would rather have you lie, saying "No you're not," than agree with her. (HCCAA, 2011)

- Sometimes when the congregation is invited to sing, you will hear some poor or off-key singing. This is O.K. Do not say anything or make any gestures, such as covering your ears, to indicate your displeasure.

- Even though a restaurant hostess may tell you an exact length of time before you will be seated, such as 20 minutes, consider this an estimate. In reality the wait may be longer or shorter.

- If you are invited to a picnic, it is considerate to ask what the host would like you to bring. (HCCAA, 2011)

- If your friend asks, "Would you like to have this?" and then offers you a snack or treat from a multiple-servings package, she is not intending you to eat everything in the package. Help yourself to a reasonable serving if you wish.

- Bringing a Weight Watchers™ cookbook to a birthday party for an overweight friend is not a good idea unless the friend has specifically asked for it. It is viewed the same as calling your friend fat.

### Chapter Four:

# Important Points I've Discovered Along the Way

During my odyssey of bringing intentionality to learning the hidden curriculum, I have learned many things not only about the hidden curriculum, but about life in general. I am especially grateful because my life today is so much better. I no longer feel like each day is a chaotic surprise waiting to happen that could derail me at any moment.

So, how did I get from where I was four years ago to where I am today? There are many factors, but there are four in particular I would like to share in this section:

- the concept of critical mass,
- the realization that I don't need to report the truths in life as I see them,

- understanding and employing the concept of reattribution, and
- developing self-advocacy skills.

These ideas have each been significant aspects of life getting better for me over the past four years. By sharing them here, I hope that readers will be able to either use them or at least adapt them so they work in their own lives.

# Critical Mass

When compiling three years of hidden curriculum calendar items for this book, I noticed how similar many of the items were. At the same time, I realized it took several similar instances for my neurology to compile enough similar data for me to make sense out of it. Once I had enough data compiled, I would find that I no longer needed to intentionally remember each hidden curriculum "rule" pertaining to a specific topic such as the unruly behavior of other people's children or comments about others with the word "fat" in them.

Instead, it was as if all the individual hidden curriculum items or rules on a given subject came together in a way that made a light go on for me. Brenda Smith Myles refers to this as having enough experiences to enable you to develop a critical mass (personal communication, 2010). After this happened, I knew the information in a different sort of way. I no longer needed to even think about or try to remember the individual hidden curriculum items pertaining to the topic at hand. Instead, it was as if those items had somehow morphed into my general operating system. I no longer needed to intentionally go on a search-and-find mission to uncover a pertinent hidden curriculum item in order to act on the previous information I had learned and stored.

Another thing I noticed when compiling literally thousands of learned hidden curriculum items was that once there was enough critical mass on a given topic, such as racism, for example, so that the information became part of my operating system, similar topics, in this case, sexism, had also morphed into my operating system even though I had not intentionally noticed and compiled information on sexism.

It was necessary for me to learn, item-by-item, many similar, but not exactly identical, items until I had stored enough individual items to create a critical mass. I needed to enter enough data for the critical mass to develop, and once the individual data morphed into a critical mass, it automatically became part of my operating system.

The following is a list of similar items, but when I was in the process of learning the individual items, they did not at all seem similar to me. Now that these items have morphed into critical mass, I no longer need to remember each one individually. In fact, they are automatically a part of me, and I realize from them a general rule not to make comments about people's bodies. I don't always get it right, but I get it right frequently enough so that I no longer hide from other people to avoid social embarrassment.

In short, they are examples of individual items adding up over time to produce a critical mass, which then enabled me to "just know" that any negative comment about another's body would be likely to get me into social trouble.

## Hidden Curriculum Items: Body Comments

- Even though you may mean it as a compliment, telling someone they are too flimsy could be perceived as a negative comment.

- Sometimes people lose a significant amount of weight. Even though it may indeed look like their butt fell off, it is better not to say so. This sort of comment will likely not be perceived as a compliment.

- Sometimes older people have grayish or yellowish teeth. Even though you think their teeth would look better if they used a teeth-whitening product, it is rude to tell them so. Sharing this sort of truth hurts people's feelings.

- Even though you may be concerned that being overweight will have negative effects on the health of a friend, do not tell her how to go about losing weight unless she specifically asks for this information.

- Even if strangers with a small child look old enough to be the child's grandparents, don't refer to them as grandma or grandpa. If they are the parents, they will not appreciate it being pointed out they look old enough to be the child's grandparents.

- It is best not to ask a woman when her baby is due without knowing for sure she is pregnant. When you assume a woman is pregnant and she is not, even though you have not said "you look fat," she will interpret your message this way and likely experience hurt feelings over your comment.

- Do not touch a pregnant woman's belly or a bald man's head unless the person is your significant other.

- Though you may know exactly how many wrinkles a person has on her face, it is best not to even mention it.

- It is rude to announce to people that they stink because you think that the smell of their perfume or cologne is too strong. If you are made uncomfortable by it, try to remove yourself from the situation.

- It is fine to notice you are sweating, but it is not the sort of information others will want to know. Therefore, do not announce it.

- It is an unwritten rule that it is not O.K. to comment on physical quali- ties such as wrinkles and gray hair.

- It is generally considered rude to comment on any unfavorable bodily smell such as sweat, but complimentary to comment on favorable body smells such as perfume.

- Sometimes when riding on a plane you will find yourself with a large seatmate whose body spills over into your seat. You may ask the attendant to change seats. Unfortunately, if the plane is full, you will just have to squeeze in and manage as best as you can. Do not say anything to the fat passenger about it.

- At a social gathering, even though you may be quite pleased that you are obviously not the heaviest person in the room, do not announce it. Doing so could make the really overweight people feel uneasy at hav- ing attention drawn to their size.

- It is O.K. for overweight people to eat dessert. Do not comment.

I repeated the following activity – intentionally watching for examples of the hidden curriculum numerous times with new experiences – and it has served me well!

**ACTIVITY:** Consider engaging in a repeating experi- ence of your own, such as going to a gym, mall, movie, bowling alley, and so on. Each time you repeat the chosen activity, intentionally watch to see what hidden curriculum items you might discover. Start your own list to keep track of the new items you discover.

Here are some hidden curriculum rules I was able to discover
in different areas merely by seeking out novel-to-me activities
and intentionally observing for the purpose of discovering all
the hidden social rules I could.

## Hidden Curriculum Items: At the Gym

- If you do not feel comfortable changing in front of others in a public locker room, you may change your clothes in the restroom. (HCCAA 2010)

- In a public locker room, put a towel on the bench before setting your naked body down. This is a socially mandatory hygiene practice.

- If you step out of the shower at the gym and discover you have forgotten to bring a towel, it is better to use your gym shirt or pants as a towel than to get dressed without drying off at all.

- In a public locker room, some people shower with their swimsuit on; others don't. Either way is fine.

- For sanitary reasons, if you have to go to the bathroom while in a swimming pool, get out and go to the restroom. (HCCAA 2010)

- If you work out at a gym, you may be asked to bring sneakers that you only wear in the gym. This is because street shoes often damage gym floors. (HCCAA 2010)

- Singing in the shower is fine at home, but it is not usually done in a public shower such as at a swimming pool or a gym. (HCCAA 2011)

- Sometimes gyms are crowded, and you may not be able to use a particular machine when you would like. It is not appropriate to tell the person using the machine that it is your turn to use it now. You will need to wait. The only exception is if a time limit is posted. Then you can politely remind a person who has exceeded the time. (HCCAA 2011)

- In a public locker room such as at a swimming pool or gym, people change clothes in front of others. It is best not to look at them when they are changing clothes even if you are talking with them. If you just "have to" look, do so sneakily enough so that nobody will notice. (HCCAA 2011)

- If you use a public locker room with built-in combination locks, be sure to give the lock dial a few spins after closing the locker door. If you don't, others may be able to open it. (HCCAA 2011)

## Hidden Curriculum Items: Sporting Events

- Comments about "chewing up the clock" or "eating the clock" during football games mean the team in possession of the ball is executing plays that run down the clock time. This can happen near half time or the end of the game when the team with the ball is in the lead.

- If you aren't sure when to cheer at a sporting event, a good rule of thumb is to cheer when the crowd cheers using the same words you hear others saying.

- Concession vendors at a baseball game are not like waitresses or waiters in a restaurant. You cannot order something for them to bring to you. If you want something they are not toting on their tray, you must go to the concession stand to purchase it.

- People do not like to watch sports games with persons who get angry or who dwell on a lost game for hours after the game is over. Even though you may hate to see your favorite team lose, express your feelings and then stop talking about it.

- If you are a spectator at a child's sports game, don't yell negative remarks. If you don't have something positive to say, keep your comments to yourself. (HCCAA 2011)

- When the national anthem is played at a baseball game or sporting event, people remove their hats and stand to sing. If you would rather not sing, that's O.K., but standing and removing your hat is socially mandatory. (HCCAA 2011)

- When spectators sit on bleachers at crowded sporting events, the sides of their bodies usually touch the person next to them. Even if you hate sitting like this, you cannot expect others to give you more space. Don't even ask. (HCCAA 2010)

- Some baseball players spit on the ground because they chew tobacco. Other adults generally do not spit on the ground. In fact, in most places it is considered ill mannered to do so. (HCCAA 2011)

# It Is Not Necessary to Report All My Truths!

It is not always necessary to say what you know when you see others not observing the hidden curriculum. In fact, it is usually best not to do so!

Since I had to intentionally learn the hidden curriculum, to this day I still need to remind myself that this isn't the case with NTs. For the most part, they automatically learn it. In fact, even though I can now recognize social missteps in their behavior (only because I had to painstakingly learn it), most NTs do not respond favorably when I share my knowledge.

This took me a long time to understand, because all my life, even during all my adult years and to this day, people take it upon themselves to tell me whenever I socially misstep. Sometimes even strangers have done so, publicly yelling at me. At other times, close friends let me know in much kinder ways when I make social missteps and graciously supply the missing item of the hidden curriculum for me.

However, there seems to be a hidden curriculum double standard. Even though it is socially acceptable for NTs to point out hidden curriculum violations committed by autistics, it is NOT socially acceptable for autistics to point out hidden curriculum violations committed by NTs. I have found that if I share this information in the same manner my friends have shared my mess-ups with me, unlike them, I am not considered a "good" person for having done so. For the most part, when I report to NTs that they are messing up socially, I am thought of as a rude, obnoxious or ungrateful person. (I know this because I have been told so by various NTs.)

I realize this is a generalization; yet, it makes me sad that this is often the case. I think it is because even though we may not think of it, there is an unwritten social hierarchy of the importance or goodness of human beings. I think it is because autistics do not measure up socially due to the ways autism plays out in our brains, and the resulting behavior that is often socially different is sometimes defined by the majority as socially deviant.

Rather than debating the rightness or wrongness of this fact, I realize that this is part of the process of autistics coming into their own, so to speak, both as individuals and as a culture. I think it grand to be living at this time in history and to be able to see and be a part of adult autistics taking their place in the world.

Here is a list of hidden curriculum items that I have learned it is generally not a good idea to inform NTs about, even though it is likely considered by society, at this point in history, to be perfectly O.K. for NTs to inform autistics when these sorts of social violations are committed.

## Hidden Curriculum Items: No Need to Report or Comment On

- You may find smoking a disgusting habit, but do not share this information with strangers you see smoking. To smoke or not to smoke is a personal choice. (HCCAA 2011)

- Sometimes when people talk, you can see a little bit of spit flying out of their mouth. Even though it is impolite to spit on people, it is also considered impolite to comment on this situation. Go figure!

- "Go figure" is an expression of puzzlement over some seeming contradiction.

- Even though it is wrong to drop food wrappers or other litter on the ground, it is not wise to remind a stranger who just littered. You never can tell how someone might react and, besides, it isn't any of your business.

- Sometimes people who do not appear to have a disability use the disability-labeled stall in a public restroom. Do not comment about this.

- Even though it may be unsanitary to share makeup, some people do. This is a personal choice, and you should not comment or try to get them to change their ways on this.

- Even though you may believe it is a sin to waste food, it is never acceptable to insist others eat all the food on their plates. In addition, people generally do not care that you think wasting food is a sin, so don't mention it.

- Sometimes friends share a dessert in a restaurant. Each person uses her own fork or spoon to eat some of one serving. It is fine not to participate but if choose not to, do it without any comments about sanitation, sharing germs and possible diseases.

- Some people send out holiday cards. Others don't. You are free to do whatever you wish with regard to sending out cards.

- People do not reuse Christmas cards. If you are going to send Christmas cards, you must use new cards. This is not the time to recycle.

- If you are part of a group of carolers, know that it is O.K. if some of the singers are a bit off key. In fact, it is best not to point it out.

- Some people attend parties on New Year's Eve, some people stay home and watch TV to see the ball drop in Time's Square at midnight and some people go to bed as usual. It is fine to spend the evening any way you wish.

- You may choose not to use hand driers in public restrooms if the sound bothers you, but you cannot expect others to refrain from using them. In fact, it would be considered out of line to ask them not to use them.

# The Power of Reattribution

Learning about attribution theory from reading Sherry Moyer's ECLIPSE Model (Moyer, 2009) was extremely helpful to me in my quest to learn more hidden curriculum. Sherry defines attribution as "our ability to accurately assign cause and effect or motivation to another person's thoughts, words, or deeds, or to the events around us. In other words, it is our ability to connect the dots between the events that happen to us and the reasons why they happen" (p. 32).

The way we assess our circumstances is what is referred to as the process of attribution. That is a cognitive process carried out across three parameters: locus of causality (internal, external), stability (stable, unstable) and controllability (controllable, uncontrollable) (Moyer, 2009).

Reading this gave me a great feeling of power because up until this time, I had felt pretty helpless with regard to my ability to become an "adequate" human being in the eyes of society. Understanding these parameters, I began to see that a lifetime of my own faulty attribution had led to the negative and powerless way I thought about myself.

It is a relief to now have a way to evaluate situations that used to leave me feeling as if others hated me. For example, when I was seated at a restaurant right next to the swinging door to the kitchen, my first thought was, "How can that waitress hate me so much? She somehow knows I am a bad person and, therefore, has placed me in this busy, noisy area." Using the three parameters of assessing circumstance, I came to understand that where I had been seated had to do with available seating in the moment rather than being a personal vendetta against me and that if I preferred a different seat I could ask to wait until another table was available. Here is how I sorted out the information.

**My assumption:** The waitress seated me next to the kitchen because she could somehow tell I was a bad person and, therefore, hated me.

After I decided to apply the three parameters of attribution, my thinking changed.

**Causality:** When I looked at causality, I could see that where I was seated didn't have anything to do with the kind of person the waitress thought I was (internal causality) but had to do with the open tables in the restaurant at the time (external causality).

**Stability:** With regard to stability, which tables were available would change as people finished eating and left the restaurant. This meant that if I wanted to wait, my choice of tables would change.

**Controllability:** In the moment, the only table available was the table next to the noisy kitchen where I would need to put up with the swinging door. However, if I waited until some customers left the restaurant, I would be able to sit at their vacated table. In that sense, I had control over the situation if I wanted to wait. Also, I could choose simply not to eat at that restaurant and to leave.

Using these three parameters helped me see that the situation was not hopeless – I was not a bad person AND I could do something about the situation. When the waitress returned with my water, I asked if I might be moved to another table as soon as one opened up because the swinging door was bothersome to me. She was very accommodating and moved me in a short time.

This explanation of reattribution parameters laid out in the ECLIPSE Model gave me a tremendous tool to use in my own life. It did not teach me the hidden curriculum, but it gave me a concrete way to examine the everyday interactions I had with people, which for the most part left me with the hopeless feeling of being an inadequate human being. When I began applying Moyer's reattribution information as in the above example, I started to see myself as a more adequate human being. This in and of itself allowed me an ever-increasing willingness to engage with more and more people, including strangers. By doing so I was able to learn about the hidden curriculum at an ever-increasing rate.

✱**ACTIVITY:** Think of a circumstance you have been in where you thought something happened because someone disliked or hated you. Using the outline below, think of the three parameters of attribution. You may ask a trusted friend or family member to help think through this with you so as to get more ideas. Also, you can look at my example above.

_____ happened because _____ dislikes or hates me.

**Causality** (internal, external):

**Stability** (stable, unstable):

**Controllability** (controllable, uncontrollable):

The following are some of the hidden curriculum items I was able to learn by applying reattribution.

## Hidden Curriculum Items: Reattribution

- If you perceive that someone's comment about you was mean and wish to check it out, rather than accusing the person of being mean, you might ask, "Why would you say something like that?" This will give the person an opportunity to explain. (HCCAA 2011)

- When the doctor asks, "What can I do for you today?" you are meant to only talk about the health concerns that brought you to the doctor's office in the first place.

- If you are a customer making a complaint, you will likely get better results if you use a pleasant voice to state your complaint. You don't need to be unpleasant in order to be assertive and firm. (HCCAA 2011)

- Sometimes couples kiss dramatically in public places. Regardless of what you think about this, it is best not to make any comment at all.

- Sometimes entrees in different restaurants have the same name but taste and look completely differently. It is not appropriate to accuse a restaurant of false advertising when this happens.

- At dessert time, even though you ate too much and feel like throwing up, nobody will want to know. It is sufficient to say you are too full for dessert,

- Always thank people who give you a gift, whether you like the gift or not. You are thanking them for their thoughtfulness in thinking enough of you to give you a gift. (HCCAA 2010)

- Even though you may be against swatting flies, you cannot expect others to refrain from swatting flies. In fact, it may be best to not even talk about it.

- When the dentist asks you to open your mouth to rinse, etc., even though he may be asking, it is not to indicate you have a choice. Instead it is a way to let you know what is expected. Also, there is no need to answer even though his direction may be posed as a question.

- There are lots of reasons why people laugh. They are not always laughing at you. (HCCAA 2010)

- Everyone occasionally makes mistakes. This does not indicate a major character flaw. (HCCAA 2011)

- When conversing with somebody and the other person says, "excuse me," it is usually an indication that he or she didn't hear what you said. (HCCAA 2011)

# The Role of Self-Advocacy

During the time I was intentionally trying to learn the hidden curriculum, I had the honor and privilege of meeting other adults
on the autism spectrum at national autism conferences. At one
such conference, I heard Valerie Paradiz speak on self-advocacy. As soon as her book *The Integrated Self-Advocacy ISA™*
*Curriculum: A program for emerging self-advocates with autism*
*spectrum and other conditions* (2009) came out, I read it from
cover to cover. I was so excited to finally have something that
told me exactly how to become a self-advocate.

Up until that time, it had been my experience that NTs in
autism circles automatically referred to and called me a self-
advocate. I never understood the assumption that if an adult
has autism, he or she somehow is a self-advocate. I had no
idea what it meant or how to do it but understood it was the
expectation others had about me and about my involvement
as a person with autism in autism groups.

To me it seemed logical that every human being is a self-advocate, but I reasoned that maybe because autistics are not good
at it, the NTs thought if they assigned this attribute to us that we
would magically start to self-advocate. One time I even asked
someone in an autism group, "Do you use the term self-advocate to describe me to underline the fact that I stink at it and
point out that you expect me to get better at it?"

Also, I thought self-advocacy had something to do with poli-
tics because the term was usually used in conjunction with

wanting to "get some of our self-advocates to the capitol." I was not interested in loud, noisy, crowded political demonstrations at the state capitol and, therefore, thought that self-advocacy wasn't for me!

Then I heard Valerie Paradiz speak, and that perception began to change. I learned about how to scan my environment, develop a plan and turn my plan into action. Doing

this made a very significant impact on my life. It allowed me a proactive way to navigate many socially novel situations. Because of consistently using the ideas from *The Integrated Self-Advocacy ISA™ Curriculum: A program for emerging self-advocates with autism spectrum and other conditions* (even before it was published), I am now able to go pretty much anywhere and to speak to any-size crowd, comfortably navigating most of the social situations that come up when doing so. I would not be able to do the work I do today if I had not come across the direct teaching in *The Integrated Self-Advocacy Curriculum ISA™*.

## Hidden Curriculum Items: Self-Advocacy

- If you are asked if you would like to play cards with a group of people, it is O.K. to ask what card game they play and if there will be money involved (betting) before deciding to accept or decline the invitation. (HCCAA 2011)

- If flash photography is painful to your eyes, it is fine to say so and politely decline to be photographed at social gatherings if someone asks to take your picture. (HCCAA 2011)

- Fireworks celebrations are loud, and usually the crowd is large. Be prepared, because once at the event, there are not many accommodations possible. (HCCAA 2011)

- If the crowds associated with holiday gatherings become overwhelming for you, plan ahead of time how you will enjoy the gatherings while taking care of your needs. Often, just being in a quiet room for short periods of time is helpful. (HCCAA 2011)

- Many people wear perfume or cologne to dress-up events such as concerts and plays. Be prepared to cope silently. This is something you cannot change. (HCCAA 2010)

- Being good friends means that occasionally you will each participate in an activity that may not be your favorite. You do this because it is important to the other person. It is considerate to do this without complaining. (HCCAA 2010)

- The PA systems in public places such as airports and outdoor fairs are often loud. If this bothers you, be prepared with earplugs or ear buds to attach to an iPod. However, it is still important to be aware of what is going on around you.

- If you prefer not to wash your hands in a public restroom, you could carry a small personal-sized bottle of hand sanitizer to use instead.

- It is best to look at a person who greets you and return the greeting. If looking into someone's eyes is painful for you, try glancing at the person's forehead to serve the same purpose. (HCCAA 2011)

- If you prefer no other passenger to occupy the seat next to you on a bus, you can signal this by placing something such as a shopping bag, newspaper or purse on the seat. If the bus becomes crowded, be considerate and remove the item to make room for another passenger.

- Most times, you will have to wait beyond the scheduled time of a medical appointment. Plan on this and be prepared to pass the time quietly. You can bring a book to read, an iPod or something else you can quietly do. (HCCAA 2011)

- Never agree to meet someone you have chatted with in an Internet chat room in a private place for the initial face-to-face meeting. Instead, meet in a public place where there are people around. It is best to bring a friend along also. (HCCAA 2011)

## Conclusion:

# Effectively Living My Life as an Autistic Adult

**A**s relayed throughout this book, it took me several years
of intentionally seeking out new social situations, looking for the hidden curriculum all around me and questioning
others about it before I acquired enough individual hidden
curriculum items for a critical mass to develop. During that
time, I was also applying attribution theory and intentionally
training myself in self-advocacy. All these things – reattribution, self-advocacy and developing critical mass – taken
separately are powerful. The fact that I was learning them *at
the same time* seemed to have an exponential synergistic effect. I believe this effect provided the impetus for a dramatic
change in my life.

During the three years of writing hidden curriculum calendar content, I have become a much more socially competent person. Even though my autism remains an integral part of who I am as a person, learning the hidden curriculum has allowed me the joy and freedom to take my place in the world, developing many new relationships, and my life has become better than it ever was before. If I can learn everything recorded in this book after age 50 and wind up with a much better life, I have hope that other autistics can do the same! Indeed, nobody is ever too old to learn to become more socially competent if that is something they desire.

I do not know any adult service provider that routinely teaches autistic clients the hidden curriculum, even though knowing and understanding the hidden curriculum is necessary for social competence. Indeed, lack of social competence is often the deal breaker in keeping a job, maintaining a home and forging relationships with others – the stuff of a satisfying quality of life for most of us.

In conclusion, even though I have still not cracked the code, I have been able to chisel away at it enough to feel more comfortable in my life lived out in this world as an autistic. I guess this boils down to mean that even though I will always view the world through my autistic neurology, in all the important things of life I am more like a typical human being than I am different.

## Conclusion

Regardless of our understanding of the hidden curriculum and the resulting mannerisms and behaviors, I believe that at the end of the day, we all want to feel comfortable in our own skin, loving and being loved, while engaged in the business of living our lives in community with one another. Through intentionally learning the hidden curriculum, I have gained new access to the wide world on the other side of my skin.

# References

Endow, J. (2009). 2010 *Hidden curriculum one-a-day calendar for older adolescents and adults: Items for under-standing unstated rules in social situations.*

Endow, J. (2010). *2011 Hidden curriculum one-a-day calendar for older adolescents and adults: Items for under-standing unstated rules in social situations.*

Grandin, T. (1995, 2006). *Thinking in pictures: My life with autism.* New York, NY: Vintage Books, a Division of Random House, Inc.

Grandin, T., & Barron, S. (2005). *The unwritten rules of social relationships.* Arlington, TX: Future Horizons.

Moyer, S. (2009). *The ECLIPSE model: Teaching self-regulation, executive function, attribution, and sensory awareness to students with Asperger Syndrome, high-functioning autism, and related disorders.*

Myles, B. S. (2006). *2007 Hidden curriculum one-a-day calendar: Items for understanding unstated rules in social situations.*

Myles, B. S., & Duncan, M. (2007). *2008 Hidden curriculum one-a-day calendar: Items for understanding unstated rules in social situations.*

Myles, B. S., & Duncan, M. (2008). *2009 Hidden curriculum one-a-day calendar: Items for understanding unstated rules in social situations.*

Myles, B. S., Trautman, M. L., & Schelvan, R. L. (2004). *The hidden curriculum: Practical solutions for understand-ing unstated rues in social situations.* Future Horizons.

Paradiz, V. (2002). *Elijah's cup: A family's journey into the community and culture of high-functioning autism and Asperger's Syndrome.* New York, NY: The Free Press.

Paradiz, V. (2009). *The integrated self-advocacy ISA™ curriculum: A program for emerging self-advocates with autism spectrum and other conditions.*

# References

Purkis, J. (2006). *Finding a different kind of normal.* Philadel-
phia, PA: Jessica Kingsley Publishers.

Williams, D. (1996). *Like color to the blind.* New York, NY:
Times Books, a division of Random House.

Willey, L. H. (1999). *Pretending to be normal: Living with Asperger's Syndrome.* London: Jessica Kingsley Publishers, Ltd.

# *What Others Say ...*

"In *Learning the Hidden Curriculum*, Judy Endow provides an easy-to-understand process and a wealth of suggestions for how to deal with social situations. While social rules are complex and often hard to interpret, Judy uses her usual wit and thoughtfulness in unraveling the complexity. This is an incredibly helpful book for individuals on the autism spectrum and for those who are helping them navigate the social world."
> – Cathy Pratt, PhD, BCBA-D, director, Indiana Resource Center for Autism

"The unique value of this resource is that it speaks directly to the intelligence, honesty and integrity of the many individuals with autism with whom I've had the pleasure to work. Often, the biggest challenges faced by parents and educators in teaching the 'hidden curriculum' to older children and teens is communicating *why* it is important to adjust one's perspective to interact more successfully in the neurotypical world. Judy clearly and respectfully communicates the empowering impact that this 'code-cracking' skill can have for an individual with autism in navigating social situations with self-confidence and self-control. I will be buying multiple copies of this book to use with teachers, students and parents. I can't wait to get it into the hands of the many people whose lives will be positively impacted by its message."
> – Lisa E. Combs, MA, president, Combs Educational Consulting, Ltd., and coordinator, Miami Valley Regional Autism Coaching Team, Dayton, Ohio

"While the title refers to the 'odyssey of one autistic adult,' I believe it describes in varying degrees the odyssey of all autistic adults and a few neurotypicals as well. The personal strategies and techniques that Judy presents in this brilliant book reminded me of aspects of my own journey as an autistic adult through the maze of the hidden curriculum. She describes what I have come to refer to as autistic social maps that I and others on the spectrum use to emulate what neurotypicals seem to do naturally. I highly recommend this book."
> – Malcolm B. Mayfield, manager, Autism STAR

"Lack of social competence is often the deal breaker in getting and keeping a job, maintaining a home and forging relationships with others – the stuff of a satisfying quality of life for most of us. Judy provides us with specific examples and strategies to assist in the learning, teaching and needed intentionality of addressing the hidden curriculum. All educators should read this excellent book. You will come away with new insights as a result."

> – Mary Summers, EdD, liaison to the IDEA Partnership, American Association of School Administrators

"What is particularly heartening about Endow's book is its demonstration that the window of opportunity for learning life's 'hidden curriculum,' which eludes many children and adolescents with autism, does not close after the teenage years. Judy Endow kept learning and eventually achieved 'a critical mass' that enabled her to generalize from the thousands of specific rules for expected behavior that she had been acquiring. Finally, the hidden curriculum was no longer hidden!"

> – Shirley Cohen, PhD, professor emeritus, Hunter College of the City University of New York, and author of *Targeting Autism*

"*Learning the Hidden Curriculum: The Odyssey of One Autistic Adult* provides a format for adults on the autism spectrum to assess where they are in navigating the hidden social curriculum. Judy Endow speaks candidly about the discoveries of her journey, and invites readers to reflect on their own personal experiences via activities. The section on the power of reattribution contains information that is essential to the development and maintenance of young adults' sense of self-worth. In reading it, I got excited as I considered how this book might be used as a guide for middle school and high school students in our schools. I plan to share this book as a resource in my autism and transition planning and parent workshops."

> – Thomasina Maxwell Howe, MS, director, Office of Autism, NYC Dept. of Education, District 75

*"Learning the Hidden Curriculum: An Odyssey of One Autistic Adult* offers a structure for understanding and teaching social competency. Acknowledging that people often become aware of social norms through mistakes, Judy Endow gives readers permission to forgive themselves of these mistakes, but then challenges them to move forward to develop the skills necessary to avoid future mishaps. The book offers a comfortable balance between acceptance of the social challenges associated with autism and an expectation for striving to develop competencies to move forward to a meaningful adult life."

– Chris Filler, RN BSN, coordinator, OCALI Lifespan Transitions Center (Ohio Center for Autism and Low Incidence), parent of young man with autism and co-author of *OCALI Transition to Adulthood Guidelines for Individuals With ASD*

---

**Judy Endow, MSW,** maintains a private practice in Madison, Wisconsin, providing consultation for families, school districts, and other agencies. Besides having autism herself, she is the parent of three grown sons, one of whom is on the autism spectrum. Judy conducts workshops and presentations on a variety of autism-related issues, is part of the Wisconsin DPI Statewide Autism Training Team, and is a board member of the Autism Society of America, Wisconsin Chapter. Her first book, *Making Lemonade – Hints for Autism's Helpers* (CBR Press, 2006), shows how Judy has used the lemons of her autism to "make lemonade" in her own life. Judy is also the author of *Outsmarting Explosive Behavior – A Visual System of Support and Intervention for Individuals with Autism Spectrum Disorder, Paper Words, Discovering and Living with My Autism,* the award-winning DVD *The Power of Words,* the 2010 and 2011 *Hidden Curriculum One-A-Day Calendar for Older Adolescents and Adults* and *Practical Solutions for Stabilizing Students With Classic Autism to Be Ready to Learn – Getting to Go!* Judy brings a great depth of understanding and compassion to her work.

Did you like this book?

Rate it and share your opinion!

**BARNES&NOBLE**
BOOKSELLERS
www.bn.com

**amazon**.com

## Not what you expected? Tell us!

Most negative reviews occur when the book did not reach expectation. Did the description build any expectations that were not met? Let us know how we can do better.

Please drop us a line at info@fhautism.com.
Thank you so much for your support!

**FUTURE        HORIZONS**

Printed in the USA
CPSIA information can be obtained
at www.ICGtesting.com
JSHW011653131023
49952JS00003B/7